AF363234

disha
Nurturing Ambitions

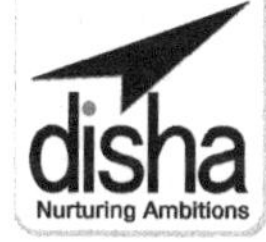

Rapid General Knowledge 2020

- **Corporate Office :** 45, 2nd Floor, Maharishi Dayanand Marg,
  Corner Market, Malviya Nagar, New Delhi-110017
  Tel. : 011-49842349 / 49842350

Typeset by Disha DTP Team

For further information about the books and ebooks from DISHA,

Log on to **www.dishapublication.com**
or email to **info@dishapublication.com**

CONTENTS

CURRENT AFFAIRS

WHO'S WHO

President – Shri Ram Nath Kovind
Vice President – Shri Venkaiah Naidu
Prime Minister – Shri Narendra Modi

List of Cabinet Ministers in India

Prime Minister	Ministry
Shri Narendra Modi	Prime Minister and also in-charge of: Ministry of Personnel, Public Grievances and Pensions; Department of Atomic Energy; Department of Space; and All important policy issues; and All other portfolios not allocated to any Minister.

		Cabinet Ministers
S. No.	**Name**	**Ministers**
1	Shri Rajnath Singh	Ministry of Home Affairs
2	Smt. Sushma Swaraj	Ministry of External Affairs
3	Shri Suresh Prabhu	Ministry of Commerce and Industry, Ministry of Civil Aviation
4	Shri Arun Jaitley	Ministry of Finance, Ministry of Corporate Affairs
5	Shri Nitin Jairam Gadkari	Ministry of Road Transport and Highways, Ministry of Shipping, Ministry of Water Resources
6	Shri D.V. Sadananda Gowda	Ministry of Statistics and Programme Implementation
7	Sushri Uma Bharati	Ministry of Drinking Water & Sanitation
8	Dr. Harsh Vardhan	Ministry of Science and Technology Ministry of Earth Sciences Ministry of Environment, Forest and Climate Change
9	Shri Ram Vilas Paswan	Ministry of Consumer Affairs, Food and Public Distribution
10	Smt. Maneka Sanjay Gandhi	Ministry of Women and Child Development
11	Shri Ananth Kumar	Ministry of Chemicals and Fertilizers Ministry of Parliamentary Affairs
12	Shri Ravi Shankar Prasad	Ministry of Electronics and Information Technology Ministry of Law and Justice
13	Shri Jagat Prakash Nadda	Ministry of Health and Family Welfare
14	Shri Chaudhary Birender Singh	Ministry of Steel
15	Shri Anant Geete	Ministry of Heavy Industries and Public Enterprises
16	Smt. Harsimrat Kaur Badal	Ministry of Food Processing Industries
17	Shri Narendra Singh Tomar	Ministry of Rural Development, Ministry of Panchayati Raj, Ministry of Mines

18	Shri Jual Oram	Ministry of Tribal Affairs
19	Shri Radha Mohan Singh	Ministry of Agriculture & Farmers Welfare
20	Smt. Smriti Zubin Irani	Ministry of Textiles
21	Shri Thaawar Chand Gehlot	Ministry of Social Justice and Empowerment
22	Shri Prakash Javadekar	Ministry of Human Resource Development
23	Shri Dharmendra Pradhan	Ministry of Petroleum and Natural Gas, Ministry of Skill Development and Entrepreneurship
24	Shri Piyush Goyal	Ministry of Coal,Ministry of Railways
25	Smt. Nirmala Sitharaman	Ministry of Defence
26	Shri Mukhtar Abbas Naqvi	Ministry of Minority Affairs

MINISTERS OF STATE (INDEPENDENT CHARGE)

S. No.	Name	Ministers
1	Shri Inderjit Singh Rao	Ministry of Planning
2	Shri Santosh Kumar Gangwar	Ministry of Labour and Employment
3	Shri Shripad Yesso Naik	Department of Ayurveda, Yoga and Naturopathy, Unani, Siddha and Homoeopathy (AYUSH)
4	Dr. Jitendra Singh	Ministry of Development of North Eastern Region
5	Dr. Mahesh Sharma	Ministry of Culture
6	Shri Giriraj Singh	Ministry of Micro, Small and Medium Enterprises
7	Shri Manoj Sinha	Ministry of Communications
8	Col. Rajyavardhan Singh Rathore	Ministry of Youth Affairs and Sports, Ministry of Information and Broadcasting
9	Shri Raj Kumar Singh	Ministry of Power, Ministry of New and Renewable Energy
10	Shri Hardeep Singh Puri	Ministry of Housing and Urban Affairs
11	Shri Alphons Kannanthanam	Ministry of Tourism

MINISTERS OF STATE

S. No.	Name	Ministers
1	General (Retd.) V.K. Singh	Ministry of External Affairs
2	Shri Inderjit Singh Rao	Ministry of Chemicals and Fertilizers
3	Dr. Jitendra Singh	Department of Atomic Energy, Department of Space Ministry of Personnel, Public Grievances and Pensions,Prime Minister's Office
4	Dr. Mahesh Sharma	Ministry of Environment, Forest and Climate Change
5	Shri Ram Kripal Yadav	Ministry of Rural Development
6	Shri Haribhai Parthibhai Chaudhary	Ministry of Mines, Ministry of Coal
7	Shri S.S. Ahluwalia	Ministry of Electronics and Information Technology

8	Shri Hansraj Gangaram Ahir	Ministry of Home Affairs
9	Shri Manoj Sinha	Ministry of Railways
10	Shri P.P. Chaudhary	Ministry of Law and Justice, Ministry of Corporate Affairs
11	Shri Upendra Kushwaha	Ministry of Human Resource Development
12	Shri Radhakrishnan P	Ministry of Shipping, Ministry of Finance
13	Shri Kiren Rijiju	Ministry of Home Affairs
14	Shri Krishan Pal	Ministry of Social Justice and Empowerment
15	Shri Vijay Sampla	Ministry of Social Justice and Empowerment
16	Shri Vishnu Deo Sai	Ministry of Steel
17	Shri Sudarshan Bhagat	Ministry of Tribal Affairs
18	Shri Vijay Goel	Ministry of Parliamentary Affairs, Ministry of Statistics and Programme Implementation
19	Shri Jayant Sinha	Ministry of Civil Aviation
20	Shri Babul Supria (Babul Supriyo) Baral	Ministry of Heavy Industries and Public Enterprises
21	Sadhvi Niranjan Jyoti	Ministry of Food Processing Industries
22	Shri Ramdas Athawale	Ministry of Social Justice and Empowerment
23	Shri Ramesh Chandappa Jigajinagi	Ministry of Drinking Water & Sanitation
24	Shri Rajen Gohain	Ministry of Railways
25	Shri Parshottam Rupala	Ministry of Agriculture & Farmers Welfare, Ministry of Panchayati Raj
26	Shri M.J. Akbar	Ministry of External Affairs
27	Shri Jasvantsinh Sumanbhai Bhabhor	Ministry of Tribal Affairs
28	Shri Arjun Ram Meghwal	Ministry of Parliamentary Affairs, Ministry of Water Resources
29	Shri Mansukh L. Mandaviya	Ministry of Road Transport and Highways, Ministry of Shipping, Ministry of Chemicals and Fertilizers
30	Smt. Anupriya Patel	Ministry of Health and Family Welfare
31	Shri C.R. Chaudhary	Ministry of Consumer Affairs, Food and Public Distribution, Ministry of Commerce and Industry
32	Dr. Subhash Ramrao Bhamre	Ministry of Defence
33	Shri Ajay Tamta	Ministry of Textiles
34	Smt. Krishna Raj	Ministry of Agriculture & Farmers Welfare
35	Shri Shiv Pratap Shukla	Ministry of Finance
36	Shri Ashwini Kumar Choubey	Ministry of Health and Family Welfare

37	Dr. Virendra Kumar	Ministry of Women and Child Development, Ministry of Minority Affairs
38	Shri Anant kumar Hegde	Ministry of Skill Development and Entrepreneurship
39	Shri Gajendra Singh Shekhawat	Ministry of Agriculture & Farmers Welfare
40	Dr. Satya Pal Singh	Ministry of Human Resource Development, Ministry of Water Resources

HEADS OF ORGANIZATIONS AND IMPORTANT POSITION HOLDERS IN INDIA

Department / Position	Person
Attorney General of India	K. K. Venugopal
Central Vigilance Commissioner	K V Chowdary
Chairman, ISRO	Kailasavadivoo Sivan
Chairman, LIC	V K Sharma
Chairman, SBI	Rajnish Kumar
Chairman, NABARD	Harsh Kumar Bhanwala
Chairman, NASSCOM	Rishad Premji
Chairman, Press Council of India	Chandramauli Kumar Prasad
Chairman, Press Trust of India	Viveck Goenka
Chief Economic Advisor	Arvind Subramaniam (His tenure ended on June 2018, New one is yet to be selected)
Chairman, Economic Advisory Council	Bibek Debroy
Chief Election Commissioner	Sunil Arora
Chief Justice of India	Ranjan Gogoi
Chief of the Air Staff	Air Chief Marshal Birender Singh Dhanoa
Chief of the Army Staff	General Bipin Rawat
Chief of the Naval Staff	Admiral Sunil Lanba
Comptroller and Auditor General	Rajiv Mehrishi
National Security Advisor	Ajit Kumar Doval
Director, BARC	Kamlesh Nilkanth Vyas
Director, Intelligence Bureau	Rajiv Jain
Foreign Secretary (MEA)	Vijay Keshav Gokhale
Secretary (Economic Affairs)	Subhash Chandra Garg
Defence Secretary (MoD)	Sanjay Mitra
GST Council (Chairman)	Arun Jaitley (Finance Minister)
GST Council (Secretary)	Hansmukh Adhia (Revenue Secretary)
GST Council (Commissioner)	Shashank Priya & Dheeraj Rastogi
Bombay Stock Exchange (Chairman)	Sethurathnam Ravi
Bombay Stock Exchange (MD & CEO)	Ashish Kumar Chauhan
National Stock Exchange (Chairman)	Ashok Chawla
National Stock Exchange (MD & CEO)	Vikram Limaye

President, CII	Rakesh Bharti Mittal
President, FICCI	Rashesh Shah
Principal Scientific Adviser	Prof K. Vijay Raghavan
Spokesperson, MEA	Raveesh Kumar

HEADS OF REGULATORY BODIES OF VARIOUS SECTORS IN INDIA

Sector	Regulator	Current Head	Est.
Telecom	Telecom Regulatory Authority of India (TRAI)	Ram Sevak Sharma (Chairman)	1997
Financial Audit and Accounting	Institute of Chartered Accountants of India (ICAI)	Naveen ND Gupta (President)	1949
Financial System and Monetary Policy	Reserve Bank of India (RBI)	Urjit Patel (Governor)	1935
Security Market	Security and Exchange Board of India (SEBI)	Ajay Tyagi (Chairman)	1992
Insurance	Insurance Regulatory and Development Authority (IRDA)	Subhash Chandra Khuntia (Chairman)	1999
Company related matters	Registrar of Companies (ROC)	Arun Jaitley (Minister)	1956
Pension	Pension Fund Regulatory and Development Authority (PFRDA)	Hemant G Contractor (Chairman)	2003
Fair market	Competition Commission of India (CCI)	Devender Kumar Sikri (Chairman) Sudhir Mittal (Chair Person)	2003
Foreign Exchange and Money Laundering	Enforcement Directorate (ED)	Sanjay Kumar Mishra (Director)	1956

HEADS OF ORGANIZATIONS AND IMPORTANT POSITION HOLDERS IN THE WORLD

Department / Position	Person
Commonwealth, Head	Queen Elizabeth II
Commonwealth, Secretary-General	Patricia Scotland (F)
Federal Reserve, Chair	Jerome Powell
FIFA, President (President)	Giovanni Vincenzo Infantino (Swiss)
International Court of Justice, President	Abdulqawi Yusuf (Somalia)
International Cricket Council, Chairman	Shashank Manohar
International Cricket Council, CEO	David Richardson
International Labor Organization (ILO), Director-General	Guy Ryder
International Monetary Fund (IMF), Managing Director	Christine Lagarde (F)

International Olympic Committee, President	Thomas Bach
INTERPOL, President	Meng Hongwei (Term ended in 2018)
INTERPOL, Acting President	Kim Jong Yang (Senior VP)
INTERPOL, Secretary-General	Jürgen Stock
NASA, Administrator	Jim Bridenstine
OPEC, Secretary-General	Mohammed Sanusi Barkindo
SAARC, Secretary-General	Amjed Hussain B. Sial
UNESCO, Director-General	Audrey Azoulay (F)
UNICEF, Executive Director	Henrietta H. Fore
United Nations (UN), Secretary-General	António Guterres
World Bank, Chief Economist	Pinelopi Koujianou Goldberg
World Bank, President	Jim Yong Kim
World Health Organization (WHO), Director- General	Dr Tedros Adhanom Ghebreyesus
World Trade Organization (WTO), Director- General	Roberto Azevedo

WORLD COUNTRIES, CAPITAL, LANGUAGE & THEIR CURRENCY

Country	Capital	Chief Language	Currency
Afghanistan	Kabul	Pushtu Dari	Afghani
Algeria	Algiers	Arabic, French	Algerian Dinar
Argentina	Buenos Aires	Spanish	Argentine Peso
Australia	Canberra	English	Australian Dollar
Azerbaijan	Baku	Azeri	Manat
Bahrain	Manama	Arabic, English	Bahraini Dinar
Bangladesh	Dhaka	Bangla	Taka
Belgium	Brussels	Flemish (Dutch), French, German	Euro
Bhutan	Thimphu	Dzongkha	Ngultrum
Bolivia	La Paz; Sucre	Aymara Spanish, Quechua	Boliviano
Bosnia and Herzegovina	Sarajevo	Serbo-Croatian	Conv.Mark
Brazil	Brazilia	Portuguese	Real
Bulgaria	Sofia	Bulgarian	Lev
Burkina Faso	Ouagadougou	French	Franc
Cambodia	Phnom-Penh	Khmer	Riel
Canada	Ottawa	French, English	Canadian Dollar
Chile	Santiago	Spanish	Peso
China	Beijing	Chinese (Mandarin)	Yuan
Colombia	Bogota	Spanish	Peso
Congo Formerly Zaire	Kinshasa	French	Congolese Franc
Costa Rica	San Jose	Spanish	Colon
Croatia	Zagreb	Croatian	Kuna
Cuba	Havana	Spanish	Peso

Country	Capital	Chief Language	Currency
Czech Republic	Prague	Czech	Koruna
Denmark	Copenhagen	Danish	Krone
Ecuador	Quito	Spanish	United States dollar
Egypt	Cairo	Arabic	Egyptian Pound
Ethiopia	Addis Ababa	Amharic	Birr
Fiji	Suva	English	Fijian Dollar
Finland	Helsinki	Finnish, Swedish	Euro
France	Paris	French	Euro
French Guiana	Cayenne	French	Euro
Georgia	Tbilisi	Georgian	Lari
Germany	Berlin	German	Euro
Ghana	Accra	English	Ghana Cedi
Greece	Athens	Greek	Euro
Guatemala	Guatemala City	Spanish	Quetzal
Guyana	Georgetown	English	Guyana Dollar
Haiti	Port-au-Prince	French	Gourde
Honduras	Tegucigalpa	Spanish	Lempira
Hong Kong	Victoria	English, Chinese	Hong Kong Dollar
Hungary	Budapest	Hungarian	Forint
India	New Delhi	Hindi (official), English and 22 officially recognised regional languages	Rupee
Indonesia	Jakarta	Bahasa Indonesian, Dutch, English Javanese	Rupiah
Iran	Tehran	Persian (Farsi), Turk, Kurdish, Arabic	Rial
Iraq	Baghdad	Arabic, Kurdish	Iraqi Dinar
Ireland	Dublin	Irish, English	Euro
Israel	Jerusalem	Hebrew, Arabic	Shekel
Italy	Rome	Italian	Euro
Japan	Tokyo	Japanese	Yen
Jordan	Amman	Arabic, English	Jordan Dinar
Kazakhstan	Astana	Kazakh, Russian, German	Tenge
Kenya	Nairobi	Kiswahili, English, Kikuyu	Shilling
Korea, North	Pyongyang	Korean	Won
Korea, South	Seoul	Korean	Won
Kuwait	Kuwait city	Arabic, English	Kuwait Dinar
Lebanon	Beirut	Arabic, French, English	Pound
Libya	Tripoli	Arabic	Libyan Dinar
Luxembourg	Luxembourg	French, German, English, Luxembourgish	Euro
Malaysia	Putrajaya (formerly Kuala Lumpur)	Malay, English, Chinese, Tamil	Ringgit
Mauritius	Port Louis	English, French, Creole, Hindustani	Rupee Mauritian

Country	Capital	Chief Language	Currency
Mexico	Mexico city	Spanish, Amerindian languages	Mexico Peso
Mongolia	Ulan Bator	Mangolian	Togrog
Myanmar	Naypyidar or Pyinmana (formerly Yangon)	Burmese and tribal languages	Kyat
Netherlands	Amsterdam	Dutch	Euro
New Zealand	Wellington	English and Maori dialect	New Zealand Dollar
Nigeria	Abuja	English, Hansa, Ibo, Yoruba	Naira
Norway	Oslo	Norwegian	Krone
Oman	Muscat	Arabic	Omani Rial
Pakistan	Islamabad	Urdu, Punjabi, Sindhi, Pusthu, Baluchi, Brahvi, English	Pakistani Rupee
Peru	Lima	Spanish, Quechua, Aymara	Nuero Sol
Philippines	Manila	Filipino, English, Spanish	Peso
Poland	Warsaw	Polish	Zloty
Portugal	Lisbon	Portuguese	Euro
Qatar	Doha	Arabic, English	Riyal (QAR)
Russia	Moscow	Russian	Russian ruble
Saudi Arabia	Riyadh	Arabic	Rial (SAR)
Serbia	Belgrade	Serbo-Croatian (official), Albanian	Dinar
Singapore	Singapore city	Malay, Chinese, Tamil, English	Singapore Dollar
Somalia	Mogadishu	Arabic, English, Italian	Somali Shilling
South Africa	Capetown	Afrikaans, English	Rand
Spain	Madrid	Spanish, Catalan, Basque, Galician	Euro
Sri Lanka	Colombo	Sinhala, Tamil, English	Sri Lankan Rupee
Sudan	Khartoum	Arabic, English, Dinka, Nubian	Sudanese Pound
Sweden	Stockholm	Swedish	Krona
Switzerland	Bern	German, French, Italian, Romansch	Swiss Franc
Syria	Damascus	Arabic, Kurdish, Armenian	Syrian Pound
Taiwan	Taipei	Mandarian Chinese, Taiwan, Hakka dialects	New Taiwan Dollar
Thailand	Bangkok	Thai, Chinese, English, Malay	Thai Baht
Tunisia	Tunis	Arabic, French	Dinar
Turkey	Ankara	Turkish, Kurdish, Arabic	Turkish Lira
Uganda	Kampala	English, Luganda, Swahili	Ugandan Shilling
United Arab Emirates	Abu Dhabi	Arabic	Dirham
United Kingdom	London	English, Welsh, Scots, Gaelic	Pound Sterling
United States of America	Washington D.C.	English	Dollar
Venezuela	Caracas	Spanish	Bolivar
Vietnam	Hanoi	Vietnamese, French, English, Chinese	Dong
Yemen	Sana'a	Arabic	Rial
Zimbabwe	Harare	English, Shona, Ndebela	Dollar (ZWD)

LATEST EVENTS

ISRO launches 'Young Scientist Programme' for school children

- ISRO has come up with this young scientist programme to 'catch them young'. The residential training programme will be conducted during the summer holidays. It will be held for a duration of around two weeks.
- Under the programme, three students each will be selected to participate in it every year from each state and union territory, covering CBSE, ICSE and state syllabus.
- ISRO has approached the chief secretaries of the respective states and administrators of Union Territories in India to arrange for the selection of three students from each of their states and union territories and communicate the list to ISRO.
- The eligibility for being chosen for the programme includes those students who have finished 8th standard and are currently studying in the 9th standard.
- Besides this, the selection will be based on the academic performance and extracurricular activities of the students, as per the selection criteria already circulated to the chief secretaries of the states and administrators of Union Territories.
- Each state and union territory is expected to submit the list of selected candidates to ISRO by the end of March 2019.

ISRO to launch electronic intelligence satellite 'Emisat'

- ISRO would be using a PSLV rocket with four strap-on motors. For the first time, it will be trying to orbit the rocket at three different altitudes.
- The main passenger of the PSLV rocket will be DRDO's electronic intelligence satellite 'Emisat'. The satellite alone weighs about 420 kg.
- The remaining 28 satellites would cumulatively weigh about 250 kg.
- After launching Emisat at an altitude of 763 km, the PSLV rocket will be brought down to put the 28 satellites into orbit at an altitude of 504 km.

- Following that the rocket will be brought down further to 485 km where the fourth stage will turn into a payload platform carrying three experimental payloads.
- The experimental payloads include one developed by the students of Indian Institute of Space Science and Technology, ISRO's own technology demonstrator and a Hamsat.

India's communication satellite GSAT-31 launched from French Guiana

Indian Space Research Organisation's latest communication satellite, GSAT-31 was successfully launched by Arianespace aboard its launch vehicle Ariane 5 from the spaceport in French Guiana on February 5, 2019.

The launch vehicle Ariane 5 VA-247 lifted off from Kourou Launch Base in Guiana Space Center (CSG) at 2:31 am (IST) carrying two telecommunications satellites. This is Arianespace's first launch of the year and the 103rd Ariane 5 mission.

ISRO launches Kalamsat, Microsat-R satellites on PSLV-C44 rocket

The Indian Space Research Organisation (ISRO) launched a students' satellite Kalamsat and an imaging satellite Microsat-R from the Satish Dhawan Space Centre in Sriharikota, Andhra Pradesh on January 24, 2019, marking its first launch in 2019.

The national space agency's rocket, PSLV C44 carried the satellites into the orbit.

After about 14 minutes into the flight, the rocket ejected the 700-kg Microsat R satellite at an altitude of about 277 km.

7 of the top 10 most polluted cities in the world are in India

As per the World Air Quality Report 2018 released by IQAir AirVisual and Greenpeace on March 5, 2019, seven of the top 10 most polluted cities in the world are in India.

India's Gurugram led the list of most polluted cities in the world in 2018, followed by Ghaziabad, Faridabad, Noida, and Bhiwadi in the top six worst-affected cities.

Of the 10 cities with highest pollution, seven are in India, while one is in China and two are in Pakistan.

Among the Indian cities are Gurgaon, Ghaziabad, Faridabad, Bhiwadi, Noida, Patna and Lucknow. The other three are Hotan in China and Lahore and Faislabad in Pakistan.

- Among the top 30 most polluted cities, India makes up for 22 with five in China, two in Pakistan and one in Bangladesh.
- The only non-Indian city in the top five list is Faisalabad, Pakistan.
- Delhi was ranked as the most polluted capital in the world, with Dhaka at second and Kabul at third position.
- China made a remarkable improvement since 2013 as the country's pollution levels have gone down by 40 percent. In 2013, Beijing topped the pollution charts. Beijing ranks now as the 122nd most polluted city in the world in 2018.
- In South Asia, out of 20 most polluted cities in the world, 18 are in India, Pakistan and Bangladesh.
- In Southeast Asia, Jakarta and Hanoi are the most polluted cities.
- In US and Canada, historic wildfires had a dramatic impact on air quality in August and November 2018, with 5 out of 10 most polluted cities in the world during August 2018 found in North America.

Third Indo-German Environment Forum held in New Delhi

- The one-day event involved panel discussions and parallel sessions focused on challenges, solutions and necessary framework conditions of air pollution control, waste management and circular economy as well as the implementation of NDCs and SDGs based on Paris Agreement and Agenda 2030 of UN respectively.
- It saw participation from around 250 representatives of ministries, business and science as well as non-governmental organisations.
- The forum provided an ideal platform for the bilateral exchange of high-level policy-makers and other key players on international environmental and climate policy and cooperation between the two countries.

- It was organised by the two environment ministries in cooperation with the Asia-Pacific Committee of German Business and the Federation of Indian Chamber of Commerce and Industry.

Environment Ministry launches National Clean Air Programme

- The National Clean Air Program (NCAP) aims to cut pollution in the 102 worst affected cities by 20-30 percent by 2024, taking 2017 as the base year for the comparison of PM concentration.
- The programme will be a mid-term, five-year action plan with 2019 as the first year.
- The international experiences and national studies though indicate that significant outcome in terms of air pollution initiatives are visible only in the long-term and hence the programme may be further extended to a longer time horizon after a mid-term review of the outcomes.
- The approach for NCAP includes collaborative, multi-scale and cross-sectoral coordination between the relevant central ministries, state governments and local bodies with focus on all sources of pollution.
- The interlocking of the existing policies and programmes including the National Action Plan on Climate Change (NAPCC) and other initiatives of the Government of India in reference to climate change will be done while execution of NCAP.

Textiles Minister launches scheme for development of knitwear sector

Union Minister of Textiles, Smriti Zubin Irani on February 28, 2019 launched a comprehensive scheme for the development of knitting and knitwear sector under PowerTex India in New Delhi.

The Textiles Minister also interacted with industry associations related to knit wear sector in three clusters of Kolkata, Tirupur and Ludhiana through video link. The Minister said that knitting and knitwear sector is predominantly MSME in size and mainly located in decentralised sector and is one of the major employment generator sector.

The knitting and knitwear sector has a significant contribution on the exports of textiles. Knitting is, in fact, a major segment in the entire textile value chain.

Knitted fabrics contribute to 27 per cent of the total fabric production in India and 15 per cent of knitted fabric is being exported.

GST Council reduces GST Rate on Real Estate projects

The Goods and Services Tax (GST) Council met on February 24, 2019 for its 33rd meeting and slashed GST rate on under-construction residential properties and the affordable housing projects.

- In case of non-affordable houses, the GST rate for under-construction flats and houses has been brought to 5 percent without Input Tax Credit (ITC), down from the present 12 percent.
- In case of affordable houses, the GST rate has been reduced to 1 percent without ITC from 8 percent.

Interim Budget 2019

- India is solidly back on track, marching towards growth and prosperity, and prepared the foundation for sustainable growth and better quality of life.
- The growth of the last 5 years is higher than the growth recorded by any other government since economic liberalisation.
- Inflation is a hidden and unfair tax; from 10.1% during 2009-14, inflation down to 4.6%, it was down to 2.19% in 2018.
- Fiscal deficit has been brought down to 3.4% in the revised estimates for 2018-19 and fiscal deficit is likely to be 2.5% in 2019-20.
- Farm GST has been continuously reduced, resulting in relief of Rs 80,000 crore to consumers, and most items of daily use for poor and middle class are now in the 0% to 5% tax bracket. Also, businesses with less than Rs 5 crore annual turnover, comprising over 90% of GST payers, will be allowed to return quarterly returns.
- Anti-black money measures taken have brought undisclosed income of about 1.30 lakh crore rupees to the surface. Some 3.38 lakh shell companies have so far been deregistered.
- 18% increase in direct tax collections in 2017-18, adding that 1.06 crore people have been included in the tax base. More than 1 crore citizens filed IT returns for the first time, after demonetisation.
- One lakh Digital villages planned in the next five years.
- As a tribute to Mahatma Gandhi, the world's largest behavioural change movement Swachh Bharat was initiated by my government.
- Under this more than 98% rural sanitation coverage has been achieved, and more than 5.45 lakh villages declared open defecation free. Mindset change has been achieved, it has become a Jan Andolan.
- Package of Rs. 6000 per annum for farmers with less than 2 hectares of land. Scheme will be called Pradhan Mantri Kisan Samman Nidhi.
- This scheme is along the lines of Rythu Bandhu scheme of Telangana which offers ₹10,000 per acre a year to all farmers, excluding tenant farmers and the Krushak Assistance for Livelihood and Income Augmentation (KALIA) scheme of Odisha which offers direct benefit cash transfer of ₹25,000 for a farm family over five seasons to small and marginal farmers.
- Government has announced the setting up of a 'Rashtriya Kamdhenu Aayog' to upscale the sustainable genetic upgradation of cattle resources and to enhance the production and productivity of cows. The Aayog will also look after effective implementation of laws and welfare schemes for cattle.
- Rs 750 crore has been allocated under the Rashtriya Gokul Mission (RGM) which is aimed at conserving indigenous Indian breeds of cattle through selective breeding.
- 2% interest subversion for farmers pursuing animal husbandry.
- All farmers affected by severe natural calamities will be given interest subversion for the entire period of three per cent of loans.

Middle Class

- No Income Tax for income up to Rs. 5 lakh.
- Individuals with gross income of up to Rs. 6.5 lakh will not need to pay any tax if they make investments in provident funds and prescribed equities.
- Standard tax deduction for salaried persons raised from Rs. 40,000 to Rs. 50,000.

Poor

- The Centre has allocated ₹500 crore for a new pension scheme for workers in the unorganised sector, while reducing its allocation for an existing pension scheme National Social Assistance Programme (NSAP) (a pension scheme administered by the Ministry of Rural Development) from ₹9,975 crore in the 2018-19 Budget to ₹9,200 crore for 2019-20.
- The ESI cover limit has been increased to Rs. 21,000. Minimum pension was also increased to Rs. 1000.
- Mega pension scheme for workers from the organised sector with income of less than Rs.15,000. They will be able to earn Rs. 3000 after the age of 60 years. The scheme will be called PM Shramyogi Maan Dhan Yojana.
- Workers will contribute an amount ranging from ₹55 to ₹100 each month, depending on their age, at the time of joining the scheme, while the government will deposit a matching contribution. The Centre expects 10 crore workers to get the benefit within the next five years.
- Rs 1,70,000 crore has been spent for bringing food at affordable rates to poor people. Targeted expenditure has been undertaken to improve quality of life in villages. The pace of construction of rural roads has been tripled. During 2014-18, 1.53 crore houses have been constructed under the PM Awas Yojana.
- All willing households to be provided electricity connections by March 2019.
- 25% additional seats in educational institutions to meet the 10% reservation for the poor.

Textile Sector

- Two major schemes implemented by the Ministry of Textiles — the Amended Technology Upgradation Fund Scheme and the Remission of State Levies — have seen lower allocation for 2019-20. Allocation for the textiles sector in the Interim Budget has been reduced by over ₹1,000 crore.
- Amended Technology Upgradation Fund Scheme
  - The Technology Upgradation Fund Scheme was introduced by the Government in 1999 to facilitate new and appropriate technology for making the textile industry globally competitive and to reduce the capital cost for the textile industry.
  - In 2015, the government approved "Amended Technology Upgradatio Fund Scheme (ATUFS)" for technology upgradation of the textiles industry.

RBI forms Nandan Nilekani led Committee to boost digital payments

The Reserve Bank of India (RBI) on January 8, 2018 constituted a High-Level Committee on Deepening of Digital Payments to encourage digitisation of payments and enhance financial inclusion.

The five-member committee will be headed by UIDAI's former Chairman Nandan Nilekani. The committee will review the existing status of digitisation of payments and suggest ways to bridge any gaps in the ecosystem.

The Committee will submit its report within a period of 90 days from the date of its first meeting.

Cabinet approves merger of Vijaya Bank, Dena Bank and Bank of Baroda

The Union Cabinet, chaired by Prime Minister Narendra Modi, on January 2, 2019 approved the 'Scheme of Amalgamation' for merger of Bank of Baroda, Vijaya Bank and Dena Bank.

The amalgamation will be the first-ever three-way consolidation of banks in India. The merger of Bank of Baroda, Dena Bank and Vijaya Bank was proposed by the Union Finance Ministry on September 17, 2018.

The amalgamated entity will be India's second largest Public Sector Bank and India's third largest bank with a total business of more than Rs 14.82 lakh crore.

RBI releases guidelines on Restructuring MSMEs loans

The Reserve Bank of India (RBI) on January 1, 2019 released guidelines on restructuring of advances to the Micro, Small and Medium Enterprises (MSMEs).

The central bank allowed a one-time restructuring of existing debt of up to Rs 25 crore for the MSMEs which have defaulted on payment, however, the loans given to them continue to be classified as standard assets.

The move will help MSMEs facing cash crunch in the wake of demonetisation and GST implementation.

- For restructuring of existing loans to MSMEs that are in default but 'standard' as on January 1, 2019, the RBI decided to permit a one-time restructuring without an asset classification downgrade.
- A provision of 5 percent in addition to the provisions already held shall be made in respect of accounts restructured under this scheme. However, the Banks will have the option of reversing such provisions at the end of the specified period, subject to the account demonstrating satisfactory performance.
- Post-restructuring, the Non-Performing Assets (NPAs) classification of these accounts shall be made as per the existing IRAC norms.
- Each bank or Non Banking Financial Company (NBFC) shall formulate a policy for this scheme with Board approval. The policy shall include framework for viability assessment of the stressed accounts and regular monitoring of the restructured accounts.
- Banks and NBFCs shall also make appropriate disclosures in their financial statements under 'Notes on Accounts', relating to the MSME accounts restructured under the instructions.

To be eligible for the scheme, the aggregate exposure to a borrower should not exceed Rs 25 crore as on January 1, 2019, including non-fund based facilities of banks and NBFCs.

The borrowing entity, i.e. MSME, should be GST-registered on the date of implementation of the restructuring. However, this condition will not apply to MSMEs that are exempt from GST-registration.

The restructuring has to be implemented by March 31, 2020.

President Ram Nath Kovind confers Gandhi Peace Prize for 2015, 2016, 2017 and 2018

The 2018 Gandhi Peace Prize was conferred on Yohei Sasakawa, who is at the forefront of many philanthropic initiatives. His compassionate nature can be seen in the manner in which he has worked to eliminate leprosy in India.

AWARDEES		
Year	**Awardees**	**Contribution**
2015	Vivekananda Kendra, Kanyakumari	Contribution in rural development, education, development of natural resources.
2016	Akshaya Patra Foundation and Sulabh International	Akshaya Patra Foundation was chosen for its contribution in providing mid-day meals to millions of children across India.
		Sulabh International was chosen for its contribution in improving the condition of sanitation in India and emancipation of manual scavengers
2017	Ekal Abhiyan Trust	Contribution in providing education for rural and tribal children in remote areas pan India, rural empowerment, gender and social equality
2018	Yohei Sasakawa	For his contribution in Leprosy Eradication in India and across the world

India-based 'Period. End Of Sentence' wins Best Short Documentary Oscar

The 'Period. End Of Sentence', a film on menstruation set in rural India, won the Oscar in the Documentary - Short Subject category at the 91st Academy Awards.

The film has been directed by Rayka Zehtabchi and produced by Indian producer Guneet Monga's Sikhya Entertainment. The film came into being as a part of 'The Pad Project', started by students at the Oakwood School in Los Angeles and their teacher Melissa Berton.

Award	Winner
Best Picture	Green Book
Best Actor	Rami Malek, Bohemian Rhapsody
Best Actress	Olivia Colman, The Favourite
Best Director	Alfonso Cuaron, Roma
Best Documentary – Feature	Free Solo
Best Animated Short Film	Bao
Best Documentary – Short Subject	Period. End Of Sentence

PM Narendra Modi receives Seoul Peace Prize for 2018

Prime Minister Narendra Modi on February 22, 2019 received the prestigious Seoul Peace Prize 2018 for his contribution to international cooperation and fostering global economic growth.

The committee credited him for his efforts in promoting global peace and harmony through inclusive economic growth and improving quality of life.

The award was presented to him by Kwon E-hyock, the Chairman of the Seoul Peace Prize Cultural Foundation at a grand ceremony in Seoul, South Korea. A short film on the life and achievements of Prime Minister Modi was also screened at the event.

With this, PM Modi became the 14th recipient of the Seoul Peace Prize.

Bharat Ratna 2019

The President, Ram Nath Kovind on January 25, 2019 conferred the 2019 Bharat Ratna Award, country's highest civilian honour, on former president and Congress leader Pranab Mukherjee.

The award was also conferred on RSS ideologue Nanaji Deshmukh and singer Bhupen Hazarika, both posthumously.

Congress leader **Pranab Mukherjee**, who was the 13th President of India and served from 2012 until 2017, had served under Indira Gandhi. He was also the Finance Minister under the premiership of Manmohan Singh.

Sanath Jayasuriya banned from cricket for two years

Former Sri Lankan Cricket captain Sanath Jayasuriya has been banned from cricket for a period of two years. The information was shared by the International Cricket Council through a statement on February 26, 2019.

- The 49-year-old former cricketer admitted failing to co-operate with an investigation and concealing, tampering with or destroying evidence.
- The cricketer was charged in October 2018. The charge came after a year-long investigation in Sri Lanka, where the ACU said corruption had become an inherent part of the system.
- Jayasuriya was charged after he failed to provide a phone and SIM card for the investigation after being requested by ACU.
- The statement from the ICC read that the conviction is the latest part of a much broader ICC investigation into corruption in cricket in Sri Lanka.
- It demonstrates the importance of participants in cricket, cooperating with investigations.
- The ICC had recently held an amnesty in relation to Sri Lankan Cricket resulting in eleven players and other participants coming forward with new information.
- This information has reportedly assisted in a number of ACU's ongoing investigations and has resulted in some new investigations getting underway.

Vinesh Phogat becomes first Indian athlete to be nominated in Laureus World Comeback of Year Award

Indian star wrestler Vinesh Phogat on January 17, 2019 became the first Indian athlete to be nominated for the prestigious Laureus World Comeback of the Year Award.

Vinesh has been nominated in "Laureus World Sporting Comeback" category for the year 2019 and will be competing for the award with some of the world's greatest sportspersons including golfer Tiger Woods, Canadian snowboarder Mark McMorris, American alpine ski racer Lindsey Vonn, Japanese figure skater Yuzuru Manyu and Dutch para-snowboarding star Bibian Mentel-Spee.

The Awards will be presented on February 18, 2019 in Monaco, a tiny independent city-state on France's Mediterranean coastline.

- Phogat has been nominated for the award alongside US Tour Championship winner Tiger Woods, who won his first tournament in five years.
- The 24-year-old from Haryana made a sensational comeback in 2018 after battling a long injury lay-off.
- She not only won gold at the 2018 Gold Coast Commonwealth Games but also won a silver in the 2018 Asian Championships in Bishkek and a gold at the Asian Games in Jakarta.
- Phogat was one of the favourites to win a medal for India at the 2016 Olympics in Rio de Janeiro, Brazil, but a horrific knee injury forced her out of the tournament during the quarter-finals.
- Though the injury was viewed virtually as a death sentence for her career, the wrestler steadily worked her way back to fitness.
- She won gold at the CWG and went on to dominate the field at the Asiad, dropping just two points and spending a little over 11 minutes on the mat, which took her through to the final.
- Aged just 24, she was one of the nominees for the Padma Shri award in 2018 and is expected to be a favourite to win a medal in the 2020 Tokyo Olympics.

Mary Kom becomes 'World No 1' Boxer in latest AIBA World Rankings

The celebrated MC Mary Kom became the World No 1 Boxer in 45-48 kg category in the latest International Boxing Association's (AIBA) World Rankings released on January 10, 2019.

Mary Kom was placed by AIBA at top of the charts in the 45-48 kg category weight division with 1700 points.

'Magnificent Mary' became the most successful boxer in world championships history when she claimed the 48kg category top honours in November 2018, her unprecedented sixth world title triumph.

USA announces to end preferential trade treatment to India

The United States has given India a 60-day withdrawal notice on the Generalized System of Preferences (GSP) benefits extended to $5.6 billion worth of Indian exports.

Under the GSP around 2000 Indian products get duty free access to the USA market.

Second Trump-Kim Summit

Donald Trump and Kim Jong-Un met for the second time in Vietnam following their historic first meeting in Singapore

US declares national emergency

US President Donald Trump has signed an executive order declaring national emergency in the nation to construct a wall along the US-Mexico border.

Wing Commander Abhinandan Varthaman returns

Wing Commander Abhinandan Varthaman, who was in Pakistan custody, was released at Wagah Border by Pakistani authorities amidst heightened tensions between India and Pakistan.

Foreign Minister attends OIC summit in UAE

External Affairs Minister Sushma Swaraj attended the foreign ministers' meet of the Organisation of Islamic Cooperation (OIC) in Abu Dhabi.

IAF destroyed JeM terrorist camps in POK

The Indian Air Force fighter jets crossed the line of control and destroyed Jaish-e-Mohammed terror camps in Pakistan occupied Kashmir.

Around 300 terrorists were killed during the non-military operation.

National War Memorial complex

PM dedicated the National War Memorial complex to the nation

The complex includes a central pillar, an eternal flame, and six bronze murals depicting famous battles fought by Indian Army, Air Force and Navy.

Pulwama Attack

In a worst ever terror attack in Jammu & Kashmir, 44 jawans of the Central Reserve Police Force (CRPF) were martyred and several others injured following a suicide bombing attack.

Corruptions Perception Index

In the recent global corruption index released by anti-corruption watchdog Transparency International, India is moved to 78th position and improved its old ranking of 81.

Top three countries in the list are Denmark, New Zealand and Singapore

Vande Bharat Express

India's first Semi High Speed Train, 'Vande Bharat Express' was flagged off on New Delhi-Kanpur-Allahabad-Varanasi route from the New Delhi Railway Station.

India started operations of Chabahar Port in Iran

India started operations of Chabahar port after it took over the operations of a part of Chabahar Port in Iran during the Chabahar Trilateral Agreement meeting held in December 2018.

Sheikh Hasina secured her third consecutive term

Bangladesh's PM Sheikh Hasina secured her third consecutive term with a landslide victory in the nation's general elections.

COP-24 conference

The 2018 United Nations Climate Change Conference the COP-24 Conference of the Parties to the United Nations Framework Convention on Climate Change took place in Katowice, Paris

Pravasi Bharatiya Diwas

15th Pravasi Bhartiya Diwas took place in Varanasi and around 6,000 NRIs participated in the three-day event.

CBI chief sacked

A High-powered selection committee headed by Prime Minister Narendra Modi removed Alok Verma as CBI chief.

Alok Verma announced his resignation from the services following the decision.

Kumbh 2019

The world's largest religious and cultural human congregation -Kumbh 2019 has begun with the holy dip at Sangam, the confluence of rivers Ganga, Yamuna and mythical Saraswati at Prayagraj.

Citizenship (Amendment) Bill

The Lok Sabha passed the Citizenship (Amendment) Bill.

The bill seeks to amend the Citizenship Act, 1955 to make illegal migrants of religion Hindus, Sikhs, Buddhists, Jains, Parsis and Christians from Afghanistan, Bangladesh and Pakistan, eligible for citizenship.

Merger of Banks

Union cabinet has approved the merger of Vijaya Bank & Dena Bank with Bank of Baroda. After this merger which will come into effect from 1st April 2019, Bank of Baroda will become the third biggest public sector bank.

India improves the IP Index ranking

India improved its previous position and placed at 36th rank in the recent Intellectual Property Index

New RBI Governor

Former Revenue Secretary Shaktikanta Das appointed as the twenty-fifth Governor of the Reserve Bank of India.

Doing Business Ranking

India Improves Rank by 23 Positions in Ease of Doing Business released by World Bank and placed at 77th rank among 190 countries.

25th High Court of India

The Andhra Pradesh High Court becomes the 25th high court in the country

It initially started functioning w.e.f 1st January 2019 from a temporary structure till the Permanent building comes up in the Justice City complex in the state's capital Amravati.

National Mineral Policy, 2019

The Union Cabinet has approved National Mineral Policy 2019. The policy is aimed at bringing about more effective regulation to the mining sector as well as a more sustainable approach while addressing the issues of those affected by mining.

Highlights:

- It focuses on Make in India initiative and Gender sensitivity in terms of the vision.
- National Mineral Policy 2019 replaces the National Mineral Policy 2008. In 2017, the Supreme Court had directed to review NMP 2008.
- Important features of the new policy include:
  - Introduction of Right of First Refusal for RP (Reconnaissance Permits)/PL (Prospecting Licenses) holders.
  - Encouraging the private sector to take up exploration and attract private investment through incentives.
  - Auctioning of virgin areas on a revenue sharing basis.
  - Development of online public portal with provision for generating triggers at higher level in the event of delay of clearances.
  - Encourages dedicated mineral corridors to facilitate the transportation of minerals
  - Introduces the concept of Inter-Generational Equity that deals with the well-being of present as well as future generations.
  - Proposes to constitute an inter-ministerial body to institutionalize the mechanism for ensuring sustainable development in mining.

National Housing Bank

The Cabinet has approved payment of the face value of the subscribed share capital of Rs.1450 crore in National Housing Bank(NHB) to Reserve Bank of India (RBI) consequent to amendments made to the NHB Act, 1987 in 2018.

Key Points:

- The wholesale financing role of NHB will get strengthened with the transfer of ownership to Government, thereby making possible augmented funding support to housing finance companies.
- The change in ownership from RBI to GoI will also segregate RBI's role as a banking regulator and as the owner of NHB.

FAME-India Scheme

The Union cabinet has approved the proposal for implementation of scheme titled 'Faster Adoption and Manufacturing of Electric Vehicles in India Phase II (FAME India Phase II)' for the promotion of Electric Mobility in the country.

Key Points:

- The scheme is with a total outlay of Rs 10000 Crores over the period of three years.
- It is the expanded version of the present scheme titled 'FAME India1 which was launched in April 2015.
- The scheme proposes to give a push to electric vehicles (EVs) in public transport.
- It seeks to encourage the adoption of EVs by way of market creation and demand aggregation.
- FAME India is a part of the National Electric Mobility Mission Plan. The main thrust of FAME is to encourage electric vehicles by providing subsidies.

National Policy on Software Products 2019

The Union Cabinet has approved the National Policy on Software Products 2019 to develop India as a Software Product Nation.

Highlights:

- Initially, an outlay of Rs 1500 crore is involved to implement the programmes and schemes envisaged under this policy over a period of 7 years.
- The amount will be divided into Software Product Development Fund (SPDF) and Research & Innovation Fund.

- The policy will lead to the formulation of several schemes, initiatives, projects and measures for the development of software products sector in the country as per the envisaged roadmap.
- Policy will Promote the creation of a sustainable Indian software product industry, driven by intellectual property (IP), leading to a ten-fold increase in India share of the Global Software product market by 2025.
- It will nurture 10,000 technology startups in the software product industry, including 1000 such technology startups in Tier-II and Tier-III towns and cities and generate direct and indirect employment for 3.5 million people by 2025.

Pradhan Mantri JI-VAN yojana

The Cabinet Committee on Economic Affairs has approved the 'Pradhan Mantri JI-VAN (Jaiv Indhan- Vatavaran Anukool fasal awashesh Nivaran) Yojana'.

Key Points:

- The scheme focuses to incentivise 2G Ethanol sector and support this nascent industry by creating a suitable ecosystem for setting up commercial projects and increasing Research & Development in this area.
- Apart from supplementing the targets envisaged by the Government under EBP programme, the scheme will also have the following benefits:
  - Meeting Government of India vision of reducing import dependence by way of substituting fossil fuels with Biofuels.
  - Achieving the GHG emissions reduction targets through progressive blending/ substitution of fossil fuels.
  - Addressing environmental concerns caused due to burning of biomass/ crop residues & improve the health of citizens.
  - Improving farmer income by providing them remunerative income for their otherwise waste agriculture residues.
  - Creating rural & urban employment opportunities in 2G Ethanol projects and Biomass supply chain.
  - Contributing to Swachh Bharat Mission by supporting the aggregation of nonfood biofuel feedstocks such as waste biomass and urban waste.
  - Indigenizing of Second Generation Biomass to Ethanol technologies.

Tax info exchange agreement inked between India and Brunei

India and Brunei have recently signed an agreement for the exchange of information in tax matters. The pact will enable the exchange of information, including banking and ownership information between the two countries for tax purposes. The agreement also provides for mutual assistance in the collection of tax revenue claims between both countries. The agreement will enhance mutual co-operation between India and Brunei Darussalam by providing an effective framework for exchange of information in tax matters, which will help curb tax evasion and tax avoidance.

Bancassurance Agreement signed by IDBI Bank and LIC

LIC of India and IDBI Bank Ltd. have signed a bancassurance agreement to offer LIC's insurance products through IDBI Bank's branches. Now IDBI bank will get a window to provide LIC's entire gamut of insurance offerings to the Bank's 1.80 Cr customer base spread over 1800 branches across the country. Further, the Bank will become the preferred bank for LIC premium payments and function as premium point to boost sale of LIC products. IDBI Bank is fundamentally strong, having a young, energetic and talented work force that will help in selling the LIC products. This will enable the bank to add to its revenue growth and simultaneously help LIC in increasing its Bancassurance business. It's a win-win situation for both the organisations. LIC and IDBI Bank are committed to serve the interests of all its stakeholders.

Deendayal Disabled Rehabilitation Scheme

National Conference on "Deendayal Disabled Rehabilitation Scheme (DDRS)" was held at New Delhi. The Conference was organised by the Department of Empowerment of Persons with Disabilities (DEPwD), Ministry of Social Justice and Empowerment.

Key Points:

- "Scheme to Promote Voluntary Action for Persons with Disabilities" was revised and renamed as the "Deendayal Disabled Rehabilitation Scheme (DDRS)".
- It aims to create an enabling environment to ensure equal opportunities, equity, social justice and empowerment of persons with disabilities.
- Encourage voluntary action for ensuring effective implementation of the People with Disabilities (Equal Opportunities and Protection of Rights) Act of 1995.
- Provide financial assistance to voluntary organizations to make available the whole range of services necessary for rehabilitation of persons with disabilities including early intervention, development of daily living skills, education, skill-development oriented towards employability, training and awareness generation.
- With a view to inclusion of persons with disabilities in the mainstream of society and actualizing their potential, the thrust would be on education and training programmes.

EASE (Enhanced Access and Service Excellence) reform index

Government's EASE (Enhanced Access and Service Excellence) reform index has been released.

Highlights:

- EASE index is prepared by the Indian Banking Association (IBA) and Boston Consulting Group and commissioned by the Finance Ministry.
- It is a framework that was adopted last year to strengthen public sector banks and rank them on metrics such as responsible banking, financial inclusion, credit offtake and digitisation.

- Punjab National Bank has topped the list. It is followed by Bank of Baroda, State Bank of India (SBI), and Oriental Bank of Commerce.
- The EASE Index report also noted PSU banks' strengthening of the bad-loan recovery process, pointing to the success of the Insolvency and Bankruptcy Code (IBC) in fast-tracking the resolution process.

Smart India Hackathon 2019

The 3rd edition of highly successful Smart India Hackathon initiative has been started. Smart India Hackathon 2019 is a nationwide initiative to provide students with a platform to solve some of pressing problems we face in our daily lives, and thus inculcate a culture of product innovation and a mindset of problem-solving.

Key Points:

- In SIH 2019, the students will have the opportunity to work on challenges faced within the private sector organisations and create world-class solutions for some of the top companies in the world, thus helping the Private sector hire the best minds from across the nation
- SIH is an initiative by Ministry of HRD, AICTE, Persistent Systems, i4c and Rambhau Mhalgi Prabodhini
- Involves 1 Lakh+ technical students, 3000+ technical institutions, 200+ organizations from across India
- It is world's biggest Software and Hardware hackathon

Construction Technology India (CTI)

Prime Minister has inaugurated the Construction Technology India-2019 Expo-cum-Conference in Delhi.

Key Point:

- The conference identifies proven, innovative and globally established technologies for use in the Indian context.
- Technology providers, researchers, start-ups, developers, academia, public sector agencies and other domain experts participated in the event.
- The Construction Technology India (CTI) will be a biennial event.

- National Real Estate Development Council (NAREDCO) and Confederation of Real Estate Developers' Associations of India (CREDAI) took the lead with the support of Ministry of Housing and Urban Affairs in hosting this event.

Kumbh Mela 2019

The Prayagraj Kumbh Mela 2019 has secured place in the Guinness Book of World Records for the largest crowd management; largest sanitation drive and largest painting exercise of public sites.

Key Points:

- Kumbh Mela made its way into the Guinness Records by parading 500 special buses non-stop in Prayagraj to break the record of the United Arab Emirates.
- Sanitation workers set a Guinness World Record when 10,000 of them got together for a three-minute cleaning drive at Kumbh. The event was organised by the Kumbh Mela administration and the state Health Department.
- Kumbh Mela also set a Guinness World Record for the "most contribution to a handprint painting on the theme of 'Jai Gange' in eight hours. A part of 'Paint My City' initiative, the handprint community activity saw the participation of 7,664 people from all age groups.

Centre for Disability Sports to be set up

A 'Centre for Disability Sports' will be set up at Gwalior in Madhya Pradesh. The proposal regarding setting up of it has been approved by the Government.

Key Points:

- It will be registered under the Societies Registration Act, 1860, which is to function under the name of Centre for Disability Sports.
- Improved sports infrastructure created by this Centre will ensure effective participation of Persons with Disabilities (PwDs) in sports activities and also enables them to compete at national and international levels.
- Setting up of the Centre will develop a sense of belonging in Divyangjan to facilitate their integration in society.

BOLD–QIT project

Project BOLD-QIT (Border Electronically Dominated QRT Interception Technique) under CIBMS (Comprehensive Integrated Border Management system) has been inaugurated on India-Bangladesh border in Dhubri District of Assam.

Key Points:

- BOLD-QIT is the project to install technical systems under the Comprehensive Integrated Border Management System (CIBMS), which enables BSF to equip Indo-Bangla borders with different kind of sensors in unfenced riverine area of Brahmaputra and its tributaries.
- The concept of CIBMS is the integration of manpower, sensors and command and control to improve situational awareness and facilitate quick response to emerging situations.
- Among major components of CIBMS is the 'virtual fence'. The second component is the command and control, which will help in optimum use of resources for border management.
- The implementation of this project will not only help BSF to curb all types of cross border crimes but also provide respite to the troops from round the clock human surveillance.

Swachh Bharat Gramin

The National Annual Rural Sanitation Survey (NARSS) 2018-19, conducted by an Independent Verification Agency (IVA) under the World Bank support project to the Swachh Bharat Mission Gramin (SBM-G), has found that 96.5% of the households in rural India have access to a toilet use it.

Highlights:

- The survey was conducted between November 2018 and February 2019 and covered 92040 households in 6136 villages across States and UTs of India.
- The survey used the PPS (Probability Proportion to Size) sampling methodology, which yields results within a confidence interval of 95%.
- The NARSS confirmed the Open Defecation Free (ODF) status of 90.7% of villages

which were previously declared and verified as ODF by various districts/ states.

- 1% of households were found to have access to toilets during the survey period (the corresponding figure as per the SBMG MIS in November 2018 was 96%)
- 5% of the people who had access to toilets used them.
- 7% of villages which were previously declared and verified as ODF were confirmed to be ODF. The remaining villages also had sanitation coverage of about 93%.

Transport and Marketing Assistance (TMA) for specified agriculture products scheme

The Centre has notified a scheme for Transport and Marketing Assistance (TMA) for specified agriculture products that will provide assistance for the international component of freight and marketing of agricultural produce.

Highlights:

- The scheme will be available for exporters from March 1, 2019 to March 31, 2020.
- All exporters, duly registered with relevant Export Promotion Council as per Foreign Trade Policy, of eligible agriculture products shall be covered under this scheme.
- The assistance is available for most agricultural product exports with some exceptions such as live animals, products of animal origin, milk, cream, curd, butter, buttermilk, whey, rice, wheat, tobacco and garlic.
- The assistance, at notified rates, will be available for export of eligible agriculture products to the permissible countries, as specified from time to time. The assistance shall be admissible only if payments for the exports are received in Free Foreign Exchange through normal banking channels.
- The scheme shall be admissible for exports made through EDI (Electronic Data Interchange) ports only.
- The scheme covers freight and marketing assistance for export by air as well as by sea.

Janaushadhi Diwas

7th March 2019 was celebrated as 'Janaushadhi Diwas' across India. As part of the celebrations, PM Narendra Modi interacted with owners of Janaushadhi Kendras and beneficiaries of Pradhan Mantri Bhartiya Janaushadhi Pariyojana (PMBJP) across the country.

Key Points:

- 'Pradhan Mantri Bhartiya Janaushadhi Pariyojana' is a campaign launched by the Department of Pharmaceuticals, Govt. of India, to provide quality medicines at affordable prices to the masses through special kendra's known as Pradhan Mantri Bhartiya Jan Aushadhi Kendra.
- Pradhan Mantri Bhartiya Jan Aushadhi Kendra (PMBJK) have been set up to provide generic drugs, which are available at lesser prices but are equivalent in quality and efficacy as expensive branded drugs.
- Bureau of Pharma PSUs of India (BPPI) is the implementing agency of PMBJP.

Web- Wonder Women Campaign

The Ministry of Women and Child Development hosted a felicitation event for Web Wonder Women.

Highlights:

- The Campaign has been launched by the Ministry of Women and Child Development, Government of India in association with the NGO Breakthrough and Twitter India.
- Through the campaign, the Ministry aims to recognize the fortitude of Indian women stalwarts from across the globe who have used the power of social media to run positive & niche campaigns to steer a change in society.
- The Campaign is aimed at encouraging, recognizing and acknowledging the efforts of these meritorious Women.

National Sports Federation

Ministry of Youth Affairs and Sports has granted provisional recognition to Kudo International Federation India (KIFI) as National Sport Federation with immediate effect.

Key Points:

- The recognition means granting a major role to KIFI Association for promotion and Development of Kudo sport in India.
- National Sports Federations (NSFs) are autonomous bodies registered under the Societies Registration Act 1860. The Government does not interfere in their day to day affairs.
- Government has issued guidelines imposing age and tenure limits in respect of office bearers of NSFs, including those of the Indian Olympic Association (IOA).
- These have further been reiterated in the National Sports Development Code of India, 2011, which has been made effective from 31.1.2011.

Swachh Survekshan Awards 2019

The Swachh Survekshan awards 2019 were recently conferred by President Ram Nath Kovind. Swachh Survekshan 2019 covered all urban local bodies in the country, making it the largest such cleanliness survey in the world.

Highlights:

- Indore was adjudged India's cleanest city for the third straight year. The second and third positions in the category were grabbed by Ambikapur in Chhattisgarh and Mysuru in Karnataka.
- Bhopal is country's Swachh capital.
- New Delhi Municipal Council area was given the 'Cleanest Small City' award.
- Uttarakhand's Gauchar was adjudged the 'Best Ganga Town'.
- The 'Cleanest Big City' award has been bagged by Ahmedabad, while Raipur is the 'Fastest Moving Big City'.
- Ujjain has been the adjudged the 'Cleanest Medium City' and Mathura-Vrindavan bagged the tag of the 'Fastest Moving Medium Cities'.

National Rural Economic Transformation Project

India has signed a $250 million loan agreement with the World Bank for the National Rural Economic Transformation Project (NRETP) that aims to help women in rural households shift to a new generation of economic initiatives by developing viable enterprise for farm and non-farm products.

Key Points:

- The National Rural Economic Transformation project is additional financing to the $500 million National Rural Livelihoods Project (NRLP) approved by the World Bank in July 2011.
- The project will support enterprise development programs for rural poor women and youth by creating a platform to access finance including start-up financing options to build their individual or collectively owned and managed enterprises.
- The project will involve developing financial products using digital financial services to help small producer collectives scale-up and engage with the market.
- It will also support youth skills development in coordination with the Deen Dayal Upadhyaya Grameen Kaushalya Yojana.

New Delhi International Arbitration Centre Ordinance, 2019

The Union Cabinet has approved promulgation of an Ordinance for establishing the New Delhi International Arbitration Centre (NDIAC) for the purpose of creating an independent and autonomous regime for institutionalised arbitration.

Key Points:

- In order to facilitate the setting up of NDIAC, the Ordinance envisages the transfer and vesting of the undertakings of the ICADR in the Central Government. The Central Government will subsequently vest the undertakings in NDIAC.
- NDIAC will be headed by a chairperson who has been a Judge of the Supreme Court or a Judge of a High Court or an eminent person, having special knowledge and experience in the conduct or administration of arbitration law or management, to be appointed by the Central Government in consultation with the Chief Justice of India.
- There will be two Full time or Part time Members from amongst eminent persons having substantial knowledge and experience in institutional arbitration, both domestic and international.
- Also, one representative of a recognised body of commerce and industry shall be chosen on a rotational basis as Part time Member.
- Secretary, Department of Legal Affairs, Financial Adviser nominated by the Department of Expenditure and Chief Executive Officer, NDIAC shall be ex-officio Members.

Success Mantras

How to Manage Exam Stress

Stress is a feeling of an aspirant or a person when he has to perform more than he is used to perform. **Suppose you are stressed, your body responds as you are in danger. It makes hormones to speedup your heart, breathe faster and burst your energy.**

Some stress is normal and useful for you that help to work hard and react quickly. But it happens too often and lasts for too long, it can cause health problems and hindrance in your work and performance.

Healthy ways to cope with stress

(i) Take out some time for entertainment and relaxation.

(ii) Develop or keep hobby.

(iii) Rest and sleep well.

(iv) Be positive and confident.

(v) Engage socially-reach out and build relationship with the help of-
* Reach out to a colleague who is competitive aspirant.
* Help someone in need.
* Have lunch or tea with a friend.
* Call an old friend.
* Go for a walk with like minded people

(vi) **Avoid unnecessary stress**

There are a number of stressors in life and during exam preparation that can be eliminated.
* Avoid people who stress you out,
* Take control of your environment, eg. you can turn off the T.V, can study in library, etc.

(vii) **Alter the situation.**
* Express your filling instead of bottling them up.
* Be willing to compromise.
* Manage your time better.

(viii) **Accept the things you can't change**
* Don't try to control the uncontrollable.
* Look for the upside, i.e. taking challenges as opportunities for future betterment.
* Learn to forgive.

Unhealthy ways to cope with stress

Unhealthy coping strategies may temporarily reduce stress, but they cause more damage in the long run.

egs.

(i) Smoking.

(ii) Drinking alcohol.

(iii) Taking junk or comfort food.

(iv) Sitting for hours infront of T.V. or computer.

(v) Withdrawing from family, friends, and activities.

(vi) Using pills or drugs to relax.

(vii) Sleeping too much.

How to Stay Motivated

Cracking any competitive Exam is not a short term game like 'One Day' cricket match. It is a long term game plan of preparation which needs passion to keep you motivated through out your preparation.

Stay Motivated

A. Keep off De-motivators

1. Eliminate your distractions.
2. Don't lie to yourself.
3. Overcome your weaknesses
4. Don't set multi-task at a time.
5. Don't let the past dictate your future.
6. Refuse to be a victim, i.e. kept down by life hurdles and failures.
7. Stop worrying about what is beyond your control.
8. Don't repeat your mistake.

B. Keep on Motivators

* Discover the ultimate purpose of your goal
* Make sure that your goal is under your reach.
* **See the invisible**, i.e- remind yourself of your goal 24/7 time.
* Split the final goal into sub-goal, i.e. goal of day, week, month and year.
* Target first the goal of the day to achive the goal of week, month & the year.
* **Make check** points for day, week and months to check your preparation progress.

- **Give break** in study to energise yourself.
- **Surprise** yourself by outdoor lunch, game with friend, home-cooking, etc.
- Be practical & make actionable strategy.
- **Discover** your strength.
- **Keep calm** and be pressure free.
- **Learn** from your mistake.
- **Make a plan** to target your goal. Because "If you fail to plan, you plan to fail".
- **Build a team** that target the same goal.
- **Build a support team** of winners to guide, support & motivate you at the need of hour.
- **Don't care** what others think about you and keep your momentum to reach to destination.
- **See the hurdles otherwise** (i.e. opportunities) to learn something. As **Thomas Edison** said, "I have not failed. I have just found 9,999 ways that won't work."
- **Write motivational quotes** in note-books, posters on the walls, etc.
- **Keep** a motivational role-model.
- **Listen** to motivational musics & songs.
- **Do Breathing Exercise** like yoga
- **Love** others and let others love you.

Planning for Preparation

Planning is important because it tells us how to reach our destination or goal. In the context of the general competition, planning acquires greater significance because one has to cover a comprehensive syllabus in a limited period of time. Good planning really implies maximum results with minimum efforts. And effective planning means that you work out your own mechanism for checking whether you are spending your time effectively or not. Thus, you must focus on the following for success in general competitive Examinations:

Master the Basics

As you are aware that examination bodies like UPSC, State PSC, SSC, etc. have brought changes to the examination in both the pattern and the syllabus, and **The questions are likely to test the candidate's basic understanding of all relevant issues, and ability to analyze, and take a view on conflicting socio economic goals, objectives and demands.**

Thus, you don't have to master the topics, all you need is BASIC UNDERSTANDING and the ability to analyze. Basic understanding comes from reading and re-reading. Ability to analyze what you have understood from reading comes from WRITING PRACTICE.

Start From Weak Areas

There is no syllabus in detail or specific for subject or areas for general studies (G.K.). Any question in GS prelims can be asked from anywhere, so aspirants must begin their planning and study for subject area which they are weak in or afraid the most from. When the weak areas can be overcome, a new confidence will develop that will motivate to cover up other areas/subjects easily and quicker.

Apply Intelligent Meditation in Preparation

It is very important to analyse previous questions asked in Exams and then think over all the aspects and diamensions on which questions can be formed and asked from particular topic or heading.

Prepare Your Own Notes & Mind-Map

Writing notes is very helpful in preparing for the examination, particularly when you study from different sources. Firstly, while writing notes you focus your attention in a more concentrated manner and many of these points remain in your memory if you put them on a Mind Map. Secondly, notes help you in quick revision.

Revision is the key to success

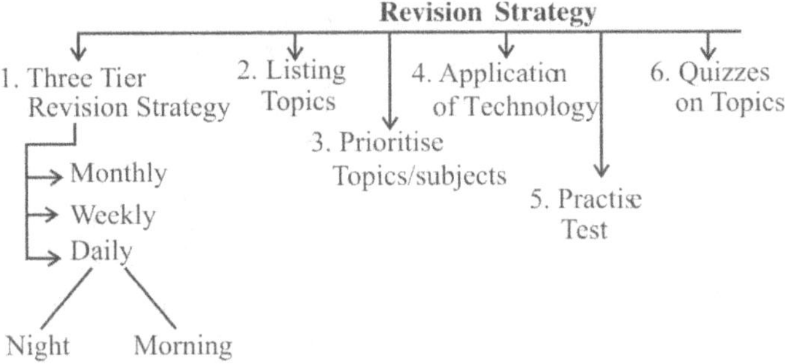

* **Revision** is the most important aspect of preparation for any exam, whether it is academic or competitive. But it plays a greater role in selection when an aspirant follows it, because of complexity of syllabus and subjects for competitive exam.

  Like study strategy, there is no fixed revision format that will suit each and every aspirant. Aspirants should think over which format can be best and suit them in revision. They can go through others revision techniques before making their own. But revision strategy should be prepared in such a way that help the aspirants to achieve their study goals in the best possible way. For examples:

1. **Three Tier Revision Strategy**

   This formate is based on three labels, i.e. day wise, week-wise and month-wise.

   Daily revision is divided into two stages, morning and late-night. In the morning, aspirants should revise quickly all the subjects, chapters and topics they have studied previous day, thereafter, they start studying new topic for the day. Before going to sleep in the late night after study, they must revise all the points they have studied the whole day.

   Weekly Revision: It is second stage of revision which covers all the topics, chapters and subjects an aspirant has studied in a week, i.e. from Monday to Saturday. It is mostly fixed on Sunday.

   Monthly Revision: Like wise weekly revision, monthly revision is the third stage of revision of the same topics and chapters which an aspirant have already revised weekly and daily in a month.

   The next revision can be after three and six months to freshen up your memory of three and six months studies. It will help the aspirants in building their confidence in preparation and cracking the exam.

General Knowledge

INDIAN PANORAMA

INDIAN STATES AND UNION TERRITORIES

India/State	Capital	Area (Sq.Km)	Language	Establish- ment Year	Sex Ratio /1000	Literacy Average %	Pop. Density (Sq. Km)	Festivals	Dance	Tribes
INDIA	New Delhi	3.3 Million	No National Language	15-08-1947	940	73%	382	G.Jayanti, I.Day. & R. Day	–	–
1. Andhra Pradesh	Hyderabad	160205	Telugu, Urdu	01-10-1953	992	67.7%	308	Sankranti, Ugadi	Kuchipudi	Andh, Bagata, Bhil, Konda
2. Arunachal Pradesh	Itanagar	83,743	English	20-02-1987	920/ 1000	66.95%	17	Losar" or The New Year	Bardo Chham	Abor, Aka, Apatani
3. Assam (Assom)	Dispur	78,550	Assamese, Bengali,	1st April 1912	–	–	397	Bihu	Ankia Naat (Onkeeya)	Mikirs, Khasis, Nagas, Boro
4. Bihar	Patna	99,200	Bhojpuri, Maithili	1st April 1936	916	63.4%	1,102	Chhath	Bidesia Kajari	Gonda, Mundas, Gaur
5. Chhattis- garh	Raipur	135,194	Chattisgarhi, Hindi	1-11-2000	991	71.04%	189	Bastar Dussehra, Bhoramdeo	Panthi, Rawat Nacha	Agariya, Andh, Baiga, Bhaina,
6. Goa	Panaji	3,702	Konkani	30-05- 1987	968	88.70%	394 per sq km.	Ganesh Chaturthi	Dekhnni, Fugdi	Dhodia, Dubla (Hal- pati),
7. Gujarat	Gandhinagar	196,204	Gujarati	01-05-1960	918	79.31%	310	Makar Sankranti	Rass-garba	Bhils, Barda, Bavacha
8. Haryana	Chandigarh	44,212	Punjabi, Haryanvi	01-11-1966	877	76.64%	573	Hariyali Teej, Lohri,	Saang, Dhamal	Meo, Ror

State	Capital	Area	Language	Date				Festivals	Dances	Tribes
9. Himachal Pradesh	Shimla	55,673	Pahari, Kangri	25-01-1971	974	83.78%	123	Kullu, Shoolini	Losar Shona Chuksam	Bhot, Bodh, Gaddi, Gujjar
10. J & K	Srinagar	222,236	Kashmiri, Urdu	26-10-1947	883	66.7%	56	Hemis, Urs	Dumhal, Rouff	Balti, Beda, Bot, Boto
11. Jharkhand	Ranchi	79,714	Santhali, Mundari, Ho	15-11-2000	947	67.6%	414	Jhumar, Paika, Chau, Agni	Karam, Vat savitri	Asur, Agaria, Baiga, Banjara
12. Karnataka	Bengaluru	191,791	Kannada	01-11-1956	968	75.60%	320	Mysore Dasara, Ugadi	Bharatanatyam, Bolak-aat	Adiyan, Barda, Bava-cha, Bhil
13. Kerala	Thiruvanantha-puram	38,863	Malayalam, English	01-07-1949	1,084	93.91%	860	Onam	Kathakali	Adiyan, Arandan
14. Madhya Pradesh	Bhopal	308,245	Hindi	01-11-1956	930	70.60%	236	Shivratri, Bahgoriya	Badhai, Rai, Saira	Bhil, Bhunjia, Biar, Binjhwar
15. Maharash-tra	Mumbai	307,713	Marathi	01-05-1960	929	82.9%	370	Vijayadashami or Dasara	Lavani, Koli	Andh, Baiga, Barda
16. Manipur	Imphal	22,327	Meiteilon	21-01-1972	987	79.21%	120	Lui-ngai-ni, Ningol Chakouba, Yaoshang	Manipuri	Aimol, Anal, Angami
17. Meghalaya	Shillong	22,429	Khasi,Garo	21-01-1972	986	75.84%	130	Nongkrem, Wangala	Nongkrem`	Chakma, Dimasa, Garo
18. Mizoram	Aizawl	21,087	Mizo	20-02-1987	975	91.58%	52	Chapchar Kut, Thalfavang Kut,	Cheraw, Khuallam	Chakma, Dimasa, Garo
19. Nagaland	Kohima	16,579	English	01-12-1963	931	80.11%	119	Hornbill, Sekrenyi	Zeliang	Naga, Kuki, Mikir, Garo
20. Odisha	Bhubaneshwar	155,820	Odia, English	01-04-1936	978	73.45%	270	Ganesh Chaturthi	Odissi	Agata, Bathudi, Birhor
21. Punjab	Chandigarh	50,362	Punjabi	15-08-1947	893	76.68%	550	Bandi Chhor, Vaisakhi, Lohri	Bhangra, Giddha	–
22. Rajasthan	Jaipur	342,239	Hindi, Rajasthani	01-11-1956	926	67.68%	201	Gangaur, Teej, Gogaji	Ghoomar	–

23. Sikkim	Gangtok	7,096	Nepali, Bhutia	16-5-1975	889	82.2%	86	Maghe, Losar	Singhi Chham	Bhutia, Lepcha, Limboo
24. Tamil Nadu	Chennai	130,058	Tamil	26-01-1950	995	80.33 %	550	Pongal	Bharata-natyam	Adiyan, Aranadan,
25. Telangana	Hyderabad	114,840	Telugu, Urdu	02-06-2014	–	66.50%	310	Ugadi	Kuchipudi	Andh, Konda
26. Tripura	Agartala	10,49169	Bengali , Kokborok	21-01-1972	961	94.65%	350	–	Goria, Jhum	Bhil, Bhutia, Chaimal
27. Uttara-khand	Dehradun	53,483	Garhwali, Kumaoni	9-11-2000	963	79.63%	189	Kandali, Ramman	Langvir Nritya	Bhotia, Buksa, Jaun-sari, Raji
28. Uttar Pradesh	Lucknow	243,286	Hindi, Urdu	01-04-1937	908	69.7%	820	Makar Sankranti, Chhath	Kathak	Bhotia, Buksa, Tharu, Baiga
29. West Bengal	Kolkata	88,752	Bengali and English	15-08-1947	947	77.08%	1,000	Durga Puja, Kali Puja	Chau dance	Asur, Baiga, Bedia, Chero
Union Territory										
1. Andaman and Nicobar Islands	Port Blair	8,073	English, Hindi	01-11-1956	878	86.27%	46	–	–	Andamanese, Chariar, Chari
2. Chandigarh	Chandigarh	114	Punjabi	01-11-1966	818	81.9%	9,300/	Lohri	Bhangra	–
3. Dadra and Nagar Haveli	Silvassa	102	English, Gujarati	11-08-1961	775	77.65%	698	Pongal	Tarpa, Bhavada	Warlis, Dublas
4. Daman and Diu	Daman	102	Gujarati, Mar-athi	30-05-1987	618	87.07%	2169	Garba	Mando, Vira	Dhodia, Dubla (Hal-pati)
5. Lakshad-weep	Kavaratti	32	English, Malayalam	01-11-1956	946	92.28%	2013	Eid-Ul-Fitr, Muharram	Lava, Kolkali	Koya, Malmi
6. NCT of Delhi	New Delhi	1,484.0	Hindi	01-02-1992	866	86.34%	11,297	Diwali, Eid ul-Fitr	–	–
7. Puducherry	Pondicherry	492	Malayalam, Tamil	07-01-1963	1,038	86.34%	2,500	Pongal	Garadi	Irulas, Villi

FOUNDATION DAY OF STATES

1st January	Nagaland Day
21st January	Manipur, Meghalaya and Tripura Day
6th Febuary	Jammu and Kashmir Day
20th February	Mizoram and Arunachal Pradesh day
11th March	Andman and Nicobar Islands Day
22nd March	Bihar Day (Bihar Diwas)
30th March	Rajasthan Day
1st April	Utkal (Odisha) Day
14th April	Tamil Nadu Day
15th April	Himachal Pradesh Day
1st May	Gujarat and Maharashtra Day
16th May	Sikkim Day
1st November	Chattisgarh
9th November	Uttaranchal (Now Uttarakhand) Day
15th November	Jharkhand Day (Jharkhand Diwas)
2nd June (2014)	Telangana Day

NATIONAL SYMBOLS OF INDIA

National Flag 	Tricolour with saffron at the top, white in the middle and India green at the bottom. The centre has a navy blue wheel with twenty-four spokes, known as the **Ashoka Chakra**. The flag is designed by **Pingali Venkayya**.
National Emblem 	The national emblem is the **Lion Capital** of **Asoka** at Sarnath which was adopted on 26th January 1950. The motto inscribed on the emblem is in **Devanagari** script: "**Satyameva jayate**" which means Truth Alone Triumphs.

National Anthem Jana Gana Mana	The anthem was composed by **Rabindranath Tagore**; adopted by the Constituent Assembly **24th January 1950.**
National Song Vande Mataram	**Vande Mataram** was composed by **Bankim Chandra Chatterjee**. It was adopted as the National song of India in **1950.**
National Flower	**Indian lotus** is the national flower. It is the representation of purity as it remains flawless despite growing in mud and water.
National Fruit	**Mango,** also known as the 'King of Fruits', is the National Fruit of India.
National River	**Ganga** is the national river of India. It is also the longest river of the country.
National Tree	The **Indian Banyan (Ficus bengalensis)** is the national tree.
National Bird	Indian **peacock** (Pavo cristatus) is the national bird of India.
National Animal	The **Tiger** known as the Lord of the Jungle is the national animal of India.
National Calendar Saka Calendar	**Saka** calendar was introduced as the National calendar by the Calendar Committee in **1957.**

Four Ends of India

Easternmost point - Kibithu:
- On river bank of **Lohit** separating India & China-Tibet.
- At altitude of 3350m in Arunachal Pradesh

Westernmost point – Ghuar Mota
In kutch, Gujarat

Temp. 45°c in Summer & 20°c in winter.
Northernmost Point –Siachen Glacier
It is J&K.
Southernmost Point
- Mainland – Kanyakumari (Cape comorin)
- India's Territory –Indira Point (Andaman & Nicobar)

CREMATORIUM OF FAMOUS PERSONS

Raj Ghat	Mahatma Gandhi	Shanti Van	Jawahar Lal Nehru
Veer Bhumi	Rajiv Gandhi	Samata Asthal	Jagjeevan Ram
Uday Bhoomi	K.R. Narayanan	Mahaprayan Ghat	Dr. Rajendra Prasad
Ekta Asthal	Giani Zail Singh, Chandra Shekhar	Karma Bhumi	Dr. Shankar Dayal Sharma
Kishan Ghat	Ch. Charan Singh	Abhay Ghat	Morarji Desai
Vijay Ghat	Lal Bahadur Shastri	Shakti Asthal	Indira Gandhi

AWARDS AND HONOURS

Prize	Field
Nobel Prize	Peace, literature, medicine, physics, chemistry, (From 1901) and economics (From 1969)
Pulitzer Prize	Journalism (From 1917)
Academy (Oscar) Awards	Film (From 1929)
Kalinga Award	Science (From 1952)
Booker Prize	Literature (From 1929)
Grammy Award	Music (From 1958)
Ramon Magsaysay Award	Government (Public) Service, Social Service, Journalism, Literature, Communication and International Understanding (From 1957)
Bharat Ratna	For outstanding contributions in the field of Art/ Literature/ Science and Public Service
Dada Saheb Phalke Award	Film (From 1969)
Jnanpith Award	Literature (From 1965)
Sarawati Samman	Literature (From 1991)
Vachaspati Samman	Sanskrit Literature (From 1992)
Shankar Award	Indian Philosophy, Culture and Art
Vyas Samman	Literature
Kabir Samman	Socio – communal Harmony
Dronacharya Award	Sports Coaching / Training (from 1985)
Arjuna Award	Sports (From 1961)
Bhatnagar Award	Science (From 1957)
Dhanwantari Award	Medical Science (From 1971)
Borlang Award	Agriculture (From 1992)

Gallantry Awards

Param Vir Chakra: The highest Gallantry Award
Mahavir Chakra: The second highest Gallantry Award
Vir Chakra: The third highest Gallantry Award
Ashok Chakra: The highest peacetime Gallantry Award
Kirti Chakra: For conspicuous Gallantry
Shaurya Chakra: For an act of Gallantry

BHARAT RATNA: THE HIGHEST CIVILIAN AWARD OF INDIA

Year	Persons
1954	Chakravarti Rajagopalachari, Dr. Sarvepalli Radhakrishnan, Dr. Chandrasekhar Venkat Raman
1955	Dr. Bhagwan Das, Dr. Mokshagundam Visvesvaraya, Pt. Jawaharlal Nehru.
1957	Pt. Govind Ballabh Pant
1958	Dr. Dhondo Keshav Karve
1961	Rajarshi Purushottam Das Tandon, Dr. Bidhan Chandra (B.C) Roy
1962	Dr. Rajendra Prasad
1963	Dr. Zakir Hussain, Dr. Pandurang Vaman (P.V.) Kane
1966	Lal Bahadur Shastri (Posthumous)
1972	Mrs. Indira Gandhi
1975	Varahagiri Venkata (V.V) Giri
1976	Kumaraswami (K.) Kamraj (Posthumous)
1980	Mary Teresa Bojaxhiu (Mother Teresa)
1983	Acharya Vinoba Bhave (Posthumous)
1987	Khan Abdul Ghaffar Khan
1988	Marudur Gopalan (MG) Ramachandran (Posthumous)
1990	Dr. Bhim Rao Ramji Ambedkar (Posthumous), Dr. Nelson Rolihlahla Mandela
1991	Rajiiv Gandhi (Posthumous), Sardar Vallabh Bhai Patel (Posthumous), Morarji Ranchhodji Desai
1992	Jehangir Ratanji Dadabhai (J.R.D.) Tata, Maulana Abul Kalam Azad (Posthumous), Satyajit Ray (Posthumous)
1997	Aruna Asaf Ali (Posthumous), Guljarilal Nanda (Posthumous), Dr. Avul Pakir Jainulabdeen (A. P.J) Abdul Kalam
1998	Madurai Sanmukhavadivu (M.S) Subbulakshmi, Chidambaram (C.) Subramaniam
1999	Prof. Amartya sen, Pt. Ravi Shankar, Loknayak Jay Prakash Narayan (Posthumous) and Gopinath Bordoloi (Posthumous)
2001	Lata Dinanath Mangeshkar, Ustad Bismillah Khan
2009	Pt. Bhimsen Gururaj Joshi
2014	Prof. CN.R. Rao, Sachin Ramesh Tenulkar (1st player and the youngest one to get 'Bhart Ratna)
2015	Atal Bihari Bajpai, Pandit Madan Mohan Malviya (Posthumous)
2019	Pranab Mukharjee, Late Nanaji Deshmukh and Late Dr. Bhupen Hazarika

Note: Lal Bahadur Shastri was the first person to be honoured with Bharat Ratna posthunously and Indira Gandhi was the first woman recipient of Bharat Ratna.

DADA SAHEB FALKE AWARD

Year	Recipient
1969	Devika Rani Roerich
1970	Birendra Nath Sircar
1971	Prithvi Raj Kapoor (Posthumously)
1972	Pankaj Mallick
1973	Sulochana (Rubi Myers)
1974	B.N. Reddy
1975	Dhiren Ganguly
1976	Kanan Devi
1977	Nitin Bose
1978	Ray Chandra (R.C.) Boral
1979	Sohrab Modi
1980	P. Jairaj
1981	Naushad Ali
1982	L.V. Prasad
1983	Durga Khote
1984	Satyajit Ray
1985	V. Shantaram
1986	B. Nagi Reddy
1987	Raj Kapoor
1988	Ashok Kumar
1989	Lata Mangeshkar
1990	Akkineni Nageshwar Rao
1991	Bhalji (Bhalchandra Govind) Pendharkar
1992	Dr. Bhupen Hazarika
1993	Majrooh Sultanpuri
1994	Dilip Kumar
1995	Dr. Rajkumar
1996	Sivaji Ganesan
1997	Kavi Pradeep
1998	B. R. Chopra
1999	Hrishikesh Mukherjee
2000	Asha Bhonsle
2001	Yash Chopra
2002	Dev Anand
2003	Mrinal Sen
2004	Adoor Gopalkrishnan
2005	Braj Bhushan Chaturvedi
2006	Shyam Benegal
2007	Manna Dey
2008	V.K. Moorthy
2009	D. Rama Naidu
2010	K. Balachander
2011	Soumitra Chatterjee
2012	Praan Krishan Sikand
2013	Gulzar
2014	Shashi Kapoor
2015	Manoj Kumar
2016	Kasinathuni Viswanath
2017	Vinod Khanna

SPORTS AWARDS

Rajiv Gandhi Khel Ratna Award

- It is India's highest honour given for achievement in sports since 1991-92.
- First Awardee 1991-92 Viswanathan Anand (Chess). Sania Mirza is for 2014-15.
- Devendra Jhajharia & Sardar Singh 2017.

Arjuna Award

- The Arjuna Awards were instituted in 1961 by the Ministry of Youth.
- From the year 2001, the award is given only in disciplines:
- Olympic Games, Asian Games, Commonwealth Games, World Cup
- World Championship Disciplines and Cricket
- Indigenous Games
- Sports for the Physically challenged

Dronacharya Award

Dronacharya Award is instituted in 1985 for sports coaching.

Dhyanchand Award

Dhyanchand Award is India's highest award for lifetime achievement in sports and games, instituted in 2002.

Founders of Indian Institutions

- **Arya Samaj**-Swami Dayanand Saraswathi
- **Athmiya Sabha**-Raja Ram Mohan Roy
- **Brahma Samaj**-Raja Ram Mohan Roy
- **Deccan Education Society**-G.G.Agarkar, M.G.Ranade, V.G.Gibhongar
- **Dharma Sabha**-Radhakanthadev
- **Indian Brahma Samaj**-Keshav Chandra Sen
- **Manavadharma Sabha**-Durgaram Manjaram
- **Prarthana Samaj**-Athmaram Pandurang
- **Pune Sewa S adan**-Smt.Remabhai Ranade, G.K.Devdhar
- **Ramakrishna Mission**-Swami Vivekananda
- **Sadharan Brahma Samaj**-Shivananda Sashtri, Anand Mohan Bose
- **Servants of India Society**-Gopalakrishna Gokhale
- **Sewa Sadan**-Bahuramji M.Malabari
- Vijayanagaram - Hariharan 1
- **Sewa Samithi**-H.N.Kunsru
- **Social Service League**-N.M.Joshi
- **Thathwabodhini Sabha**- Debendranatha Tagore
- **Theosophical Society**-Madam H.P. Blavadski, Col.H.L.Olkott

Founders of Towns in India

- Agra- Sikkandar Lodhi
- Ahmedabad - Ahmed Shah
- Ajmeer- Ajaypal Chauhan
- Allahabad- Akbar
- Culcutta- Job Charnok
- Delhi- Anankapalan
- Fathepur Sikri - Akbar
- Hisar- Ferozshah Tuglaq
- Hyderabad - Quli Qutabshah
- Jodhpur- Rao Jodha
- Mahabalipuram - Narasimhawarman
- Siri- Alaudden Khilji

FIRST IN INDIA (MALE)

First governor of Bengal	Lord Clive(1758-60)
Last governor of Bengal	Warren Hastings(1772-74)
The first British Governor General of Bengal	Lord Warren Hasting(1774-1885)
The first British Governor General of India	Lord William Bentinck(1833-1835)
The first British Viceroy of India	Lord Canning(1856-62)
The first Governor General of free India	Lord Mountbatten(1947-1948)
The first and the last Indian to be Governor General of free India	C. Rajgopalachari(1948-1950)
The first President of Indian Republic	Dr. Rajendra Prasad
The first Prime Minister of free India	Pt. Jawahar Lal Nehru
The first Indian to win Nobel Prize	Rabindranath Tagore
The first President of Indian National Congress	W.C. Banerjee
The first Muslim President of Indian National Congress	Badruddin Tayyabji
The first Muslim President of India	Dr. Zakir Hussain
The first man who introduced printing press in India	James Hicky
The first Indian to join the I.C.S	Satyendra Nath Tagore
India's first man in Space	Rakesh Sharma
The first Prime Minister of India who resigned without completing the full term	Morarji Desai
The first Indian Commander-in-Chief of India	General Cariappa

The first Chief of Army Staff	Gen. Maharaj Rajendra Singhji
The first President of India who died while in office	Dr. Zakhir Hussain
The first Prime Minister of India who did not face the Parliament	Charan Singh
The first Field Marshal of India	S.H.F. Manekshaw
The first Indian to get Nobel Prize in Physics	C.V.Raman
The first Indian to receive Bharat Ratna award	Dr. Radhakrishnan
The first Indian to cross English Channel	Mihir Sen
The first Speaker of the Lok Sabha	Ganesh Vasudeva Mavalankar
The first Vice-President of India	Dr. Radhakrishnan
The first Education Minister	Abdul Kalam Azad
The first Home minister of India	Sardar Vallabh Bhai Patel
The first chief of Army staff	K.M. Cariappa
The first Judge of International Court of Justice	Dr. Nagendra Singh
The first person to reach Mt. Everest without oxygen	Sherpa Anga Dorjee
The first Chief Election Commissioner	Sukumar Sen
The first person of Indian origin to receive Nobel Prize in Medicine	Hargovind Khurana
The first person to receive Nobel Prize in Economics	Amartya Sen
The first Chief Justice of Supreme Court	Justice Hirala J. Kania
The first Indian Pilot	J.R.D. Tata (1929)

FIRST IN INDIA (FEMALE)

The first lady to become Miss World	Reita Faria
The first woman judge in Supreme Court	Mrs. Meera Sahib Fatima Bibi
The first woman Ambassador	C.B. Muthamma
The first woman Governor of a state in free India	Sarojini Naidu
The first woman Speaker of a State Assembly	Shanno Devi
The first woman Prime Minister	Indira Gandhi
The first woman Minister in a Government	Rajkumari Amrit Kaur
The first woman to climb Mount Everest	Dachhendri Pal
The first woman to climb Mount Everest twice	Santosh Yadav
The first woman President of Indian National Congress	Annie Besant
The first woman pilot in Indian Air Force	Harita Kaur Dayal
The first woman Graduates	Kadambini Ganguly and Chandramukhi Basu, 1883
The first woman Airline Pilot	Durga Banerjee

The first woman Olympic medal Winner	Karnam Malleswari, 2000
The first woman President of United Nations General Assembly	Vijaya Laxmi Pandit
The first woman Chief Minister of an Indian State	Sucheta Kripalani
The first woman IPS officer	Kiran Bedi
The first and last Muslim woman ruler of India	Razia Sultan
The first woman to receive Ashoka Chakra	Neerja Bhanot
The first woman to cross English Channel	Arati Saha
The first woman to receive Nobel Prize	Mother Teresa
The first woman to receive Bharat Ratna	Indira Gandhi

FAMOUS NICKNAMES OF EMINENT PERSONS

Nickname	Person
Father of the Nation, Bapu	Mahatma Gandhi
Iron Man of India	Sardar Vallabhbhai Patel
Napoleon of India	Samudragupta
Shakespeare of India	Kalidasa
Mahamana	Pt. Madan Mohan Malaviya
Deshbandhu	Chittaranjan Das
Deenabandhu	C.F.Andrews
Punjab Kesari	Lala Lajpat Rai
Nightingale of India	Sarojini Naidu
Lady with the lamp	Florence Nightingale
Tota-e-Hind (Parrot of India)	Amir Khushro
Shri Guruji	M.S.Golwalkar

Superlatives : India

Structures

- **Highest Tower** (Minaret) – Qutub Minar
- **Higher Gateway** – Buland Darwaza
- **Highest Dam** – Bhakra Dam
- **Highest Bridge** – Chenab Bridge
- **Highest Airport**- Leh Air Port in Ladakh (3256 m/ 16080 ft high)
- **Highest Hydel Power Station**- Rongtong Hydel Project in Kinnaur (H.P)
- **Highest Mountain Peak**- Kanchenjunga
- **Highest Road**- Road at Khardungla in the Leh-Manali Sector

- **Highest Waterfall**- Jog Waterfall, Karnataka
- **Largest Residence** – Antilia Bhawan built by Mukesh Ambani
- **Largest Museum** – National Museum Delhi
- **Largest River Barrage** – Farakka Barrage
- **Biggest Auditorium (Mumbai)** – Sri Shanmukhanand Hall
- **Largest zoo** – Arignar Anna Zoological Park
- **Largest Cave Temple** – Ellora
- **Largest Gurudwara** – Golden Temple, Amritsar
- **Largest Mosque** – Taj-ul-Masjid at Bhopal(M.P) with area-430,000 sq. ft, & capacity 1.75 lakh people.
- **Largest Man-made Lake** – Govind Sagar (Bhakra)
- **Largest Dome** – Gol Gumbaz (Karnataka)
- **Largest Cantilever Bridge** – Howrah Bridge
- **Longest Railway Tunnel**- Pir Panjal Railway Tunnel (11 km)
- **Longest Road Tunnel** - 9.2 km long tunnel on Jammu-Srinagar National Highway
- **Largest Church**- Se Cathedral at Old Goa
- **Largest Delta**- Sunderbans (75,000 sq km)
- **Largest Stupa**- Kesariya Stupa in Bihar
- **Largest Library**- National Library, Kolkata
- **Largest Planetarium**- Birla Planetarium, Kolkata.
- **Largest Prison**- Tihar Jail, Delhi
- **Longest River Bridge** – Bandra-Worli sea link which is 5.6 km.
- **Largest Corridor** – Rameshwaram Temple Corridor
- **Largest irrigation Canal**-Indira Gandhi Canal or Rajasthan Canal (959 km long)
- **Longest Dam**-Hirakund Dam on Mahanadi river in Odisha (24.4 km long)
- **Longest Railway Bridge** – Nehru Setu Bridge (4.62 km) long
- **Tallest Statues** – Statue of Jain Saint Gomateswara at Sravanabelagola in Karnataka

- **Oldest Monastery**- Buddhist Monastery at Tawang in Arunachal Pradesh.
- **Largest mall**- Lulu Mall Kochi

Natural

- **Longest River** – Ganges
- **Largest Desert** – Thar (Rajasthan)
- **Largest Fresh Water Lake**-Kolleru in Andhra Pradesh
- **Largest Cave**- Amarnath (about 44 km from Pahalgam in Jammu and Kashmir)

SOBRIQUETS

A sobriquet is a nickname, Occasionally assumed and often given by another.

Person	Primary Names
Anna	C N Annadurai
Badshah Khan/ Frontier Gandhi	Abdul Ghaffar Khan
Buddha	Siddhartha Gautama
Chacha/Panditji	Jawaharlal Nehru
Grand Old Man of India	Dadabhai Naoroji
Gurudev	Rabindranath Tagore
Lokmanya	Bal Gangadhar Tilak
Loknayak	Jayaprakash Narayan
Man of Peace	Lal Bahadur Shastri
Netaji	Subhash Chandra Bose
Punjab kesari	Lala Lajpat Rai
Rajaji	C Rajagopalachari
Saint of the Gutters	Mother Teresa
Places	**Primary Names**
Bengal's Sorrow	Damodar Rever, India
City of Golden Temple	Amritsar, India
City of Palaces	Kolkata, India
Diamond City in India	Surat, Gujarat
Garden City of India	Bengaluru
Garden of India	Kashmir
Gateway of India	Mumbai

Pink City	Jaipur, India
Queen of Arabian Sea	Kochi, India
Spice Garden of India	Kerala
Blue Mountains	Niligiri Hills, India

Census 2011

- It is the 15th National Census survey conducted by the Census Organization of India.
- Mr. C. Chandramouli -Commissioner & Registrar General of the Census 2011.
- Survey has been conducted in 2 phases - house listing and population.
- **Population of India** – 1,210,193,422 with 623, 724, 248 males and 586,469, 174 females.

- **Total literacy rate:** 74.04%.
- **Density of population:** 382 persons/ sq.km
- **Sex ratio:** 940 females per 1000 males
- **Child sex ratio:** 914 females per 1000 males

HIGH POPULATION		
1	Uttar Pradesh	199,812,341
2	Maharashtra	112,374,333
3	Bihar	104,099,452
4	West Bengal	91,276,115
5	Andhra Pradesh	84,580,777

WORLD PANORAMA

THE NATIONAL EMBLEMS OF DIFFERENT COUNTRIES

Country	Emblem	Country	Emblem
Australia	Kangaroo	England	Rose
Barbados	Head of a Trident	Bangladesh	Water Lily
Canada	White Lily	Belgium	Lion
Denmark	Beach	Chile	Candor & Huemul
France	Lily	Dominica	Sisserou Parrot
Guyana	Canje Pheasant	Germany	Corn Flower
India	Lion Capital	Hong Kong	Bauhinia (Orchid Tree)
Ireland	Shamrock	Israel	Candelabrum
Italy	White Lily	Ivory Coast	Elephant
Japan	Chrysanthemum	Lebanon	Cedar Tree
Luxembourg	Lion with Crown	Mongolia	The Soyombo
Netherlands	Lion	New Zealand	Southern Cross, Kiwi, Fern
Norway	Lion	Pakistan	Crescent
Papua New Guinea	Bird of paradise	Spain	Eagle
Sri Lanka	Lion	Sierra Leone	Lion
Syria	Eagle	Sudan	Secretary Bird
Turkey	Crescent & Star		

NATIONAL ANIMALS OF THE MAJOR COUNTRIES

Country	Animals	Country	Animal
Afghanistan	Snow Leopard	Nepal	Cow
Albania	Golden Eagle	New Zealand	Kiwi
Australia	Kangaroo	Pakistan	Markhor
Bangladesh	Royal Bengal tiger	South Africa	Springbok
Brazil	Jaguar	Spain	Bull
Canada	North American beaver (bird)	United Kingdom	Barbary Lion
China	Giant Panda	United States	Bald Eagle
Denmark	Mute Swan	India	Bengal Tiger
Japan-bird	Green Pheasant	Kuwait	Camel
Myanmar	Tiger	Belgium	Lion

OFFICIAL BOOKS

Blue Book : An official report of the British Government
Green Book : An official publication of Italy and Persia
Grey Book : An official reports of the Government of Japan and Belgium
Orange Book : An official Publications of the Government of Netherlands
White Book : An official Publications of China, Germany and Portugal
Yellow Book : French official Book
White Paper : An official paper of the Government of Britain and India on a particular issue
Red Data Book : Russian official book which contains lists of species whose continued existence is threatened.

WORLD'S MOST POWERFUL INTELLIGENCE AGENCIES

Detective Agency	Country	Detective Agency	Country
Ministry of State Security	China	VAJA	Iran
Australian Secret Intelligence Service (ASIS)	Australia	MOSSAD	Israel
FSB	Russia	Egyption Homeland Security	Egypt
State Security Agency	South Africa	PSIA	Japan
Inter Service Intelligence (ISI)	Pakistan	Iraqi National Intelligence Service	Iraq
MI (Military Intelligence) 5 and 6, Special Branch, Joint Intelligence org.	UK	Central Intelligence Agency (CIA), Federal Bureau of investigation (FBI)	USA
Research and Analysis Wing (RAW), Intelligence Bureau (IB)	INDIA	DGSE (Direction General Dela Securite Exterieure	France

LIST OF PARLIAMENT OF DIFFERENT COUNTRIES

Country	Parliament Name	Country	Parliament Name
India	Sansad/Parliament	Maldeep	Majlis
Pakistan	National Assembly	Span	Cortes
Bangladesh	Jatiya Sansad	Nepal	Rastriya Panchayat
China	National Peoples Congress	Russia	Duma
Bhutan	Tsondu	France	National Assembly
Srilanka	Parliament of Sri Lanka	Iran	Majlis

Afganistan	Shora		Malasiya	Diwan Nigara
England	Parliament		Switzerland	Fedral Assembly
Canada	Parliament		Turkey	Grand National Assembly
Australia	Parliament			
USA	Congress			
Germany	Wondstag			
Taiwan	Yuan			
Japan	Diet			
Israil	Neset			

COUNTRIES & NEWS AGENCIES

Agency	Country	Agency	Country
Associated Press (AP)	USA	Europa Press	Spain
Allgemeiner Deutscher Nachrichtendienst	Germany	Interfax	Russia
Australian Associated Press	Australia	Islamic Republic News Agency	Iran
Agence Parisienne de Presse	France	Indonesian National News Agency	Indonesia
Antara	Indonesia	Kyodon Tsushin	Japan
Associated Israel Press (AIP)	Israel	Kenya News Agency	Kenya
Agenzia Nazionale Stampa (Associate (ANSA)	Italy	Middle East News Agency	Egypt
Associated Press of Pakistan	Pakistan	Malaysian National News Agency	Malaysia
Algemeen Nederlands	Netherlands	Novosti	Russia
Agence France Presse (AFP)	France		
Australian United Press	Australia	Press Trust of India (PTI)	India
Anadol Ajansi	Turkey	Petra	Jordan
Bangladesh Sangbad Sangstha	Bangladesh	Reuters	UK
China News Service, XinHua	China	United News of India (UNI)	India
Deutsche Presse Agentur	Germany	WAFA	Palastine
Exchange and Telegraph Company	UK		

INTERNATIONAL NEWS PAPERS

Newspaper	Place	Newspaper	Place
Al Ahram	Cairo	Mardeka	Jakarta
Bangladesh Observer	Dhaka	Mainichi Shimbun	Tokyo
China Times	Taiwan	New Statesman	U.K.
Dawn	Karachi	New York Times	New York
Daily Telegraph	U.K.	People's Daily	Beijing
Daily Mirror	London	Pravda	Moscow
Daily Mail	London	Red Flag	China
Daily News	New York	Star	Johanesberg
Eastern Sun	Singapore	Toronto Star	Canada
Ezestia	Moscow (Russia)	The Hindu	Chennei, India
Financial Times	London (U.K)	The Island	Colombo (Sri Lanka)
Independent	London (U.K)	The Times of India	India
Khaleej Times	Dubai (UAE)	The Sun	U.K.
Le Monde	Paris (France)	The Gardian	London (UK)
La Republica	Rome (Italy)	The Times	London (UK)
La Figaro	Paris (France)	Washington Post	Washington, USA

Significant Symbols or Signs

1. Black Flag — Symbol of protest
2. Flag flown at half mast — Symbol of national mouming
3. Flag flown upside down — Symbol of distress
4. A blindfolded woman holding a balanced scale — Symbol of justice
5. Black strip on face arm — Sign of mouming or protest
6. Lotus — Culture and civilization
7. Olive Branch — Symbol of peace
8. One skull on two bones crossing each other diagonally — Sign of danger
9. Pen — Symbol of culture and civilization
10. Pigeon of Dove — Symbol of peace
11. Red Cross — Medical aid and hospital
12. Red Flag — Revolution; also sign of danger
13. Yellow Flag — Flown on ships or vehicles carrying patients suffering from infectious diseases
14. White Flag — Symbol of truce
15. Wheel (Chakra) — Symbol of progress

NATIONAL MONUMENTS OF INTERNATIONAL SIGNIFICANCE

Monument	Country	Monument	Country
Statue of Liverty (New York)	USA	Leaning Tower of Pisa	Italy
Taj Mahal (Agra)	India	Emperial Palace (Tokyo)	Japan
Eiffel Tower (Paris)	France	Opera House (Sydney)	Australia
Great Wall of China	China	Kinder Disk	Denmark
Pyramid (Giza)	Egypt	Kremlin (Moscow)	Russia

IMPORTANT BOUNDARY LINES

B. Line	Between	B. Line	Between
49th Parallel	U.S.A. & Canada	Hindenburg Line	Germany & Poland
Maginot Line	Germany & France	Mannerhiem Line	Russia & Finland
Radcliffe Line	India & Pakistan	38th Parallel	North & South Korea
McMahon Line	India & China	Durand Line	Pakistan & Afghanistan

MAJOR LANGUAGES SPOKEN

Language	Speaker
Mandarin Chinese	882 million
Spanish	392 million
English	312-380 million
Arabic	206-422 million
Hindi	310 million

MAJOR RELIGIONS OF THE WORLD

Religion	Member	Percentage
Christianity	2.1 billion	33.0%
Islam	1.5 billion	21%
Hinduism	900 million	14%
Buddhism	376 million	6%
Sikhism	23 million	0.36%

INTERNATIONAL AWARDS

Nobel Prize

- It was set up in 1895 under the will of **Alfred Nobel.**
- The Nobel prizes are presented annually on 10 December (The death anniversary of the founder).
- It is given in the fields of **Peace, Literature, Physics, Chemistry, Physiology** or **Medicine** (from 1901) and **Economics** (from 1969).

Nobel Prize (Indian/ Indian origin)

1913: **Literature** – Rabindranath Tagore; was also the first Asian to win the prize
1930: **Physics** – C. V. Raman
1968: **Medicine** – Har Gobind Khorana; US citizen of Indian origin
1979: **Peace** – Mother Teresa; Indian citizen of Albanian origin
1998: **Economics** – Amartya Sen
2009: **Chemistry** – Venkatraman Ramakrishnan; US citizen of Indian origin
2014: **Peace** – Kailash Sathyarthi

Important Facts related with Nobel Prize

Unique Winners

Pierre Curie	Father (Physics)
Marie Curie	Mother (Phy, Chem)
Irene Joliot Curie	Daughter (Chemistry)

Person Refusing Nobel Prize

1931	Erik Axel Karlfeldt (Literature)
1961	Dag Hammarskjold (Peace)
1964	Jean-Paul Sartre (Literature)
1973	Le Duc Tho (Peace)

Grammy Awards

Country	United States
Presented by	National Academy of Recording Arts and Sciences
Awarded for	Outstanding achievements in the music industry
First awarded	1959

Golden Globe Awards

Country	United States
Presented by	Hollywood Foreign press Association
Awarded for	Excellence in film and television
First Awarded	1944

- **AR Rehman** is the first Indian to win Golden Globe Award in 2009 (Slumdog).

Pulitzer Prize

Country	United States
Presented by	Columbia University
Awarded for	Excellence in newspaper journalism, literary achievements and musical composition
First awarded	1917

Ramon Magsaysay Award

Country	Philippines
Presented by	Ramon Magsaysay Award Foundation
Awarded for	Outstanding contributions in six categories of government. Service, public service and other fields (Given to Asian Individuals)
First awarded	1957

India's International Awards

Mahatma Gandhi Peace Prize

It was instituted in 1995 at 125th birth aniversary and awarded by Government of India to encourage and promote Gandhian values worldwide.

- First recipient (1995): *Julius Nyerere* (Tanzania)
- Last recipient (2014): *ISRO* (India)

Jawaharlal Nehru Award

It was instituted in 1965 by Government of India for international understanding, goodwill and friendship.

- First recipient (1965) : U Thant (3rd UN Secretary-General)

- Last recipient (2009) : Angela Markel (Germany's First Female Chancellor)

Indira Gandhi Peace Prize

It was instituted in 1986 by Indira Gandhi Memorial Trust. It is awarded for peace, disarmament and development.

- First recipient (1986) : to *Parliamentarians for Global Action.*
- Last recipient (2015) : UNHCR.

World Beauty Contests

Miss World

It was created in the United Kingdom by Eric Morley in 1951. Since his death in 2000, Morley's wife, Julia Morley, co-chairs the pageant. Its headquarter is at London (UK).

Reita Faria Powell, the first Indian to win the Miss World in 1966.

Miss Universe

- It is an annual international beauty contest that is run by the Miss Universe Organisation. The contest was founded in 1952, by **California Clothing Company Pacific Mills.** Its headquarters is at **New York City (US)**.
- **Sushmita Sen** is the first Indian woman to win the Miss Universe contest in 1994.

UNITED NATIONS

Quick Facts

- **Membership:** 193 Member States
- **Established:** 24 October 1945
- **Official languages:** Arabic, Chinese, English, French, Russian, Spanish.
- **United Nations Day,** 24 October
- Based on five principal organs (formerly six–the Trusteeship Council suspended operations in 1994, upon the independence of Palau, the last remaining UN trustee territory); the **General Assembly**, the **Security Council**, the **Economic** and **Social Council (ECOSOC)**, the **Secretariat**, and the **International Court** of **Justice**.
- **General Assembly:** 193 Member States
- **Security Council:** 5 permanent members and 10 non-permanent

The Permanent Members of the Security Council

- The Peoples' Republic of China;
- The Republic of France;
- The United Kingdom of Great Britain and Northern Ireland;
- The Russian Federation; and\
- The United States of America.

The UN Flag and the Emblem

The UN General Assembly adopted the UN flag on 20 Oct. 1947. The white UN emblem is super-imposed on a light blue back ground.

Aims and Objectives

The Main objectives of the UN are :

(1) To maintain peace and security in the world.

(2) To work together to remove poverty, disease and illiteracy and encourage respect for each other's rights of basic freedom.

(3) To develop friendly relations among nations.

(4) To be a centre to help nations achieve these common goals.

SECRETARY GENERALS OF UNO AND THEIR TENURE

Name	Country	Tenure
Trigve Lie	Norway	1946-1952
Dag Hammarskjoeld	Sweden	1953-1961
U-Thant	Myanmar (Burma)	1961-1971
Kurt –Waldheim	Austria	1972-1982
Javier Perez de Cuellar	Peru	1982-1991
Boutros Boutros Ghali	Egypt	1992-1996
Kofi Annan	Ghana	1997-2006
Ban-Ki-moon	S. Korea	2007- 2 Jan, 2017
Antonio Guterres	Portugal	3 January, 2017 - till date

WORLD ORGANISATIONS AND THEIR HEADQUARTERS

Asian Development Bank (**ADB**)	Manila (Philippines)
ASEAN (Association of South –East Asian Nations)	Jakarta (Indonesia)
NATO (North Atlantic Treaty Organisation)	Brussels (Belgium)
African Union (AU)	Addis-Ababa (Ethiopia)
SAARC (South Asian Association for Regional Corporation)	Kathmandu (Nepal)
United Nations Environment Programme (**UNEP**)	Nairobi (Kenya)
International Atomic Energy Agency (**IAEA**)	Vienna (Austria)
United Nations Industrial Development Organisation (**UNIDO**)	Vienna (Austria)
UNCTAD (United Nations Conference on Trade and Development)	Geneva, Switzerland
WWF (World Wildlife Fund)	Gland (Switzerland)
International Olympic Committee (**IOC**)	Lausanne
OPEC (Organisation of Petroleum Exporting Countries)	Vienna
OECD (Organisation for Economic Co- operation and Development)	Paris
Commonwealth of Nations	London
United Nations Centre for Human Settlements (**UNCHS**)	Nairobi
United Nations International Children's Emergency Fund (**UNICEF**)	New York
United Nations Fund for Population Activities (**UNFPA**)	New York
United Nations Development Programme (**UNDP**)	New York
United Nations Institute for Training and Research (**UNITAR**)	Geneva
United Nations Research Institute for Social Development (**UNRISD**)	Geneva
World Food Programme (**WFP**)	Rome (Italy)
International Civil Aviation Organisation (**ICAO**)	Montreal (Canada)
International Fund for Agricultural Development (**IFAD**)	Rome
International Labour Organisation (**ILO**)	Geneva
International Monetary Fund (**IMF**)	Washington
Universal Postal Union (**UPU**)	Berne (Switzerland)
World Health Organisation (**WHO**)	Geneva
World Intellectual Property Organisation (**WIPO**)	Geneva
World Meteorological Organisation (**WMO**)	Geneva
Woman Aid International	London
European Free Trade Association (**EFTA**)	Geneva

SOBRIQUETS

Sobriquets Person	Primary Names
Angel of Death	Josef Mengele
Bard of Avon	William Shakespeare
Bonnie Prince Charlie	Charles Edward Stuart
Desert Fox	Erwin Rommel
Dr. Death	Jack Kevorkian
Father of his country	George Washington
Fuhrer	Adolf Hitler
Genghis Khan	Temüjin
Grand Old Man of Britain	Willian Ewart Glandstone
Honest Abe	Abraham Lincoln
Iron Lady	Margaret Thatcher
Lady with the Lamp	Florence Nightingale
Madge	Madonna
Madiba	Nelson Mandela
Maid of Orleans	Joan of Arc
Man of Destiny	Napolean Bonaparte
Old Nick	Santa
Qaid-e-Azam	Mohammad Ali Jinnah
Slick Willy	U.S. President Bill Clinton
The Bard	William Shakespeare
The Cincinnatus of the Americans	George Washington
The Duke	John Wayne
The Greatest	Muhammad Ali, Boxer
The King of Pop	Michael Jackson
The Material Girl	Madonna
The Tiger of France	Georges Clemenceau
Uncle Sam	The U.S.A.
Wizard of the North	Walter Scott

FIRST IN THE WORLD

The first person to reach Mount Everest	Sherpa Tenzing, Edmund Hillary
The first person to reach North Pole	Robert Peary
The first person to reach South Pole	Amundsen
The first religion of the world	Hinduism
The first country to print book	China
The first country to issue paper currency	China
The first President of the U.S.A	George Washington
The first Prime Minister of Britain	Robert Walpole
The first Secretary General of the United Nations	Trygve Lie
The first country to prepare a constitution	U.S.A
The first Governor General of Pakistan	Mohd. Ali Jinnah
The first person to fly aeroplane	Wright Brothers
The first person to sail round the world	Magellan
The first country to send man to the moon	U.S.A
The first country to launch Artificial satellite in the space	Russia
The first country to host the modern Olympics	Greece
The first city on which the atom bomb was dropped	Hiroshima (Japan)
The first person to land on the moon	Neil Armstrong followed by Edwin E. Aldrin
The first shuttle to go in space	Columbia
The first spacecraft to reach on Mars	Viking-I
The first woman Prime Minister of a country	Mrs. S. Bandamaike (Sri Lanka)
The first woman to climb Mount Everest	Mrs. Junko Tabei (Japan)
The first woman cosmonaut of the world	Velentina Tereshkova (Russia)
The first woman President of the U.N. General Assembly	Vijaya Lakshmi Pandit
The first man to fly into space	Yuri Gagarin (Russia)
The first batsman to score three test century in three successive tests on debut	Mohd. Azharuddin
The first U.S. President to resign Presidency	Richard Nixon

SUPERLATIVES

Tallest Animal on (land)	Giraffe
Fastest Bird	Swift
Largest Bird	Ostrich
Smallest Bird	Humming Bird
Longest Bridge (Railway)	Lower Zambeji (Africa)
Tallest Building	Burj khalifa, Dubai (U.A.E)
Longest Big Ship Canal	Seuz Canal (Linking red sea & Mediterranean)
Busiest Canal (Ship)	Baltic White Sea Canal (152 miles)
Largest Continent	Asia
Smallest Continent	Australia
Longest Day	June 21 (in Northern Hemisphere)
Shortest Day	Dec. 22(in Northern Hemisphere)
Largest Delta	Sundarbans, India (8000 sq. miles)
Longest Desert (World)	Sahara, Africa (84, 00,000 sq. km.)
Biggest Dome	Gol Gumbaz (Bijapur), (Old archi) 144 ft. diameter.
Longest Epic	The Mahabharata
Largest Island	Greenland (renamed Kalaallit Nunaat)
Largest Lake (Salt Water)	Caspian Sea 3, 71,000 sq. km.)
Largest Mosque	Masjid-al-Haram (Mecca-Saudi Arabia) Surrounds the Kaaba.
Tallest Minaret (Free Standing)	Qutub Minar, Delhi 238 ft.
Deepest & Biggest Ocean	The Pacific
Coldest Place or Region	Verkhoyansk (Syberia), Temperature – 85° C
Driest Place	Death Valley (California); rainfall 1 ½ inch.
Hottest Place (World)	Al-Aziziyah (Libya, Africa) 136°F or 57.8°C
Highest Plateau	Pamir (Tibet)
Longest Platform (Railway)	Kharagpur W.B, India (833m)
Largest Platform (Railway)	Grand Central terminal, New York (U.S.A)
Largest Port	Port of New York & New Jersey (U.S.A)
Busiest Port	Rotterdam (the Netherlands)
Longest Railway	Trans-Siberian Railway (6,000 miles Long)
Longest River	Nile (6690 km), Amazon (6570 km.)
Longest River Dam	Hirakund Dam (Orissa), India 15.8 miles.
Largest sea-bird	Albatross
Largest Sea (inland)	Mediterranean
Tallest statue	Statue of Liberty, New York (U.S.A), 150 ft. high.
Longest Swimming Course	English Channel
Longest Tunnel (Railway)	Seikan Rail Tunnel (Japan), (53.85 km.)
Longest Tunnel (Road)	Laerdal, Norway
Longest Wall	Great Wall of China (1500 miles)
Highest Waterfall	Salto Angel Falls (Venezuela)
World Rainiest Spot	Cherrapunji (Mawsynram), India
Lightest gas	Hydrogen
Hardest Substance	Diamond
Longest Animal	Blue Whale, (recorded length 106 ft. weight-195 tons)
Longest Life Span of an Animal	190 to 200 years, (Giant tortoise)
Largest Land Animal	African Bush Elephant
Fastest Animal	Cheetah (Leopard) 70 m.p.h
Longest Jump Animal	Kangaroo
Slowest Animal	Snail
Biggest Flower	Raffesia (Java)
Largest Temple	Angkor Vat (Combodia)
Largest River in volume	Amazon, Brazil
Highest Straight Dam	Bhakhra Dam
Largest Asian Desert	Gobi, Mongolia
Largest Democracy	India
Most Intelligent Animal	Chimpanzee

IMPORTANT DAYS OF THE YEAR

12th January: National Youth Day

15th January: Army Day

26th January: Republic Day

30th January: Martyr's Day

4th February: World Cancer Day

13th February: World Radio Day

14th February: St. Valentine's Day

8th March: International Women's Day and Mother's day

15th March: World Consumer Rights Day

22nd March: World Water Day

24th March: World Tuberculosis Day

7th April: World Health Day

22nd April: World Earth Day

25th April: World Malaria Day

1st May: International Labour Day

8th May: International Red Cross Day

20th May: World Refugee Day

24th May: Commonwealth Day

31st May: World No Tobacco Day

5th June: World Environment Day

8th June: World Ocean Day

21st June: International Yoga Day

23rd June: International Olympic Day

27th June: World Diabetes Day

1st July: World Doctor's Day Van Mahotsav Week (1stJuly to 7thJuly)

11th July: World Population Day

28th July: World Hepatitis Day

6th August: Hiroshima Day

12th August: International Youth Day

8th September: International Literacy Day

25th September: Social Justice Day, World Maritime Day

27th September: World Tourism Day

2nd October: Gandhi Jayanti, International Non-Violence Day

9th October: World PostalDay

16th October: World Food Day

7th November: World Cancer Awareness Day

21st November: World Television Day

3rd December: World Conservation Day

4th December: Naval Day

7th December: Flag Day

10th December: World Human Rights Day,

11th December: UNICEF Day

14th December: National Energy Conservation Day

Indian History

Sources of Ancient Indian History

- **Pliocene deposits** in Siwaliks. It is known as Ramapitheus, a type of early **hominid.**
- **Inscriptions** either on stone or on metal plates are old records of Ancient India. The study of inscriptions is called **epigraphy.**
- **Coins:** The study of coins is called **numismatics.**
    - The **Punch Mark Coins** (silver & copper) are the earliest coins of India.
- **Monuments:** Monuments reflect the material prosperity and development of culture e.g. Taxshila monuments about Kushans and Stupas, Chaityas and Vihars about Maurya.
- **Vedas:** Vedas point out features and development of different dynasties, e.g. **Rigveda** deals with Archery and known as **"The first testament of mankind."**
    - **Samveda** says about the art of music (i.e. melodies)
    - **Yajurveda:** It is known as ritual Veda.
    - **Atharvaveda:** It is the latest of the four. It is about beliefs and superstitions.
- **Upanishad:** It is anti-ritualistic in nature. It deals about the theories of creation of the universe and doctrine of action.
- **Sutras:** Sutras deal about rituals, Sanskaras, social life, Medical science etc.
- **Puranas:** Puranas describe the genealogies of various royal dynasties, i.e. Maurya, Andhra, Shishunag, Gupta, etc.
- **Jatak Kathas:** These are the parts of art and literature of 3rd century B.C.
- **Arthashastra:** It is the analysis of political and economic conditions of the Mauryas, composed by Kautilya (Chanakya).
- **Mudrarakshasa:** It tells about the establishment of the Maurya dynasty, the fall of Nanda, Ramgupta, etc.
- **Rajtarangini:** It was written by Kalhana in 12th century A.D. It is about the rulers of Kashmir. It is considered the, *"first historical book of India."*
- **Foreign travellers** wrote about the information of India. For examples –
    Megasthenes: He wrote book, "INDICA" about the dynasty of Maurya.
    Fahien: He wrote about the Gupta Emperor.

Hieun-Tsang: He wrote about the Buddhist record of the western world during period of Harshavardhan.
Albiruni: He wrote ' Tarikh-ul-Hind.'
Ibna-Batuta: He wrote about India under the rule of Muhammad Tughlaq.

Pre-Historic Period

- **Pre - historic period** is divided into three sections- **Stone age, Bronze age** and **Iron age.**
- **Stone age** is divided into three periods, i.e. Palaeolithic Age, Mesolithic Age and Neolithic Age.
- **Chalcolithic Age** is marked by the use of copper as **copper age.**
- The **Iron age** is usually associated with the **Painted Grey Wares (P.G.W.).**

Indus Valley Civilization

- The **Indus Valley Civilization (IVC)** was a unique Bronze Age civilization.
- The Civilization flourished around the Indus river basin and its tributaries, consisting of modern Pakistan and northwestern India.
- Lothal, Balakot, Suktagendor and Allahdin (Pakistan) in the cities of the Harappan civilization were the major ports.
- In the valley of the Indus people used irrigation-based agriculture.

Indus Valley Sites – Excavators
Harappa - 1921- Dayaram Sahni
Mohenjodaro- 1922- R.D.Banerjee
Sutkagendor- 1927- Aurel Stein, George
Dalesamri - 1929- M.G.Majumdar
Chanhudaro- 1931- M.G.Majumdar
Rangpur - 1931- M.S.Vats
Kot Diji- 1935- Fazal Khan
Dabarkot- 1935- Maichke
Kili Ghul Mohammad- 1950- Fairservis
Kalibangan- 1953- A. Ghosh
Ropar - 1953- Y.D.Sharma
Lothal - 1957- S.R.Rao
Surkotada- 1964- Jagatpati Ghosh
Dholvira- 1967- J.P. Joshi

The Vedic Period

- The **Vedic Period** or the Vedic Age refers to the period when the Vedic Sanskrit texts were composed in India.
- The Aryans are supposed to have migrated from Central Asia during 2000 to 1500 B.C.
- **The Rigveda** (1500–1000 BC) consists of 1028 hymns.
- The **Gaytri Mantra** had been discovered from the Rig Veda.
- The Sindhu and its tributaries are called **Sapta Sindhu.**
- The **Yajur Veda** is a book of sacrificial prayers. It is written in both verse and prose.
- The **Sama Veda** consists of **1549** hymns.
- It is a book of **chants** for singing during sacrifices.

Later Vedic Period (1000-500 BC)

- The **later Vedic** society came to be divided into four varnas called the Brahmanas, rajanyas or kshatriyas, vaisyas and shudras, each varna was assigned with its duty.

KINGDOMS OF THE LATER VEDIC PERIOD		
	Kingdom	**Location**
1.	Panchal	Bareilly, Badayun & Farrukhabad in U.P.
2.	Kushinagar	Northern region of Uttar Pradesh
3.	Kashi	Modern Varanasi
4.	Koshal	Faizabad in Uttar Pradesh
5.	Southern Madra	Near Amritsar
6.	Uttara Madra	Kashmir
7.	Eastern Madra	Near Kangra
8.	Kekaya	On the bank of Beas river east of Gandhar kingdom
9.	Gandhar	Rawalpindi & Peshawar

Chronology of Foreign Invasion

- 518–486 B.C.: King Darius or Darus invaded India.
- 326 B.C. : Alexander invaded India.
- 190 B.C. : India-Greeks or Bactrians invaded India.
- 90 D.C. : Sakas invaded India.
- A.D. 1st Century : Pahlavas invaded India.
- A.D. 45 : Kushanas or Yue-chis invaded India.

Religious Movements

Jainism

- Founder – **Rishabhadeva** (First Tirthankara).
- **Mahavira** was the last of the 24 tirthankaras.

- Jainism was divided into two sects: **Shwetambaras** and **Digambaras**.
- The **First Council** was held at **Pataliputra** by **Sthulabahu** and Second at Valabhi.

Teachings

- Jainism was based on 5 doctrines :
  (i) Ahinsa, i.e. non-violence; (ii) do not speak a lie, (iii) do not steal. (iv) do not acquire property, and (v) observe **continence** (**Brahmacharya**) introduced by Mahavira.

Three Gems of Jainism (Ratnatrya)
(i)   Right faith (Samyak Vishwas)
(ii) Right knowledge (Samyak Gyan)
(iii) Right conduct/action (Samyak Karma)

Buddhism

- Gautam Buddha was the founder of Buddhism.
- His real name was **Siddhartha**.
- His father was a king named **Suddodana Tharu** and Mother was **Mahamaya**.
- He was born at **Lumbini.**
- He discovered enlightenment under the peepal tree (**Bodhi Vriksha**) in Gaya, Bihar at the age of 35.
- He gave his first sermon at the **Deer Park in Sarnath**.
- It was divided into three main sects: Hinayana, Mahayana and Vajrayana.

Buddhist Councils

First at Rajgir, Second at Vaishali, Third at Patliputra & Fourth in Kashmir.

Important Dynasties in Ancient India

The Haryanaka dynasty(544 – 412 B.C.)

- **Bimbisara** was the first ruler and founder of Haryanka dynasty. The capital of the kingdom was **Rajagriha**.
- **Ajatasatru** who killed his father and seized the throne for himself.
- He was contemporary to Lord Mahavira and Lord Buddha and a follower of Buddhism.
- Ajatasatru was succeeded by **Udayin**.

Shishunaga dynasty (412-344 B.C.)

- The last Haryanka ruler, Nagadasaka, was killed by his courtier Shishunaga in 430 B.C, who became the king and founded the Shishunaga dynasty.

Nanda dynasty (344-321 B.C.)

- Mahapadmananda established the Nanda dynasty into a powerful empire.
- Last ruler of Nanda dynasty was Dhanananda. He was contemporary of Alexander.

- **Alexander** invasion of India took place in 326 B.C. during the reign of Dhanananda.

The Mauryan empire (322–185 B.C.)

- Founder— **Chandragupta Maurya**
- Its capital was **Pataliputra.**
- **He** embraced **Jainism**
- He died at **Sravanbelagola**
- The war of Kalinga (BC 261) was the turning point of Ashoka's life. The mass death of the war changed his mind and he became a follower of **Buddhism.**
- **Ashok Stambh** of **Sarnath** was adopted as national emblem of India.
- **Sanchi Stupa** was built by Ashoka.
- **Ashoka's Dhamma** was a code of conduct (a set of principles like respect to elders) mercy to slaves & emphasis on truth, non-violence & tolerance.

Number	Name of Emperor	Reign
1	Chandragupta Maurya	322 BC - 298 BC
2	Bindusara	298 BC - 272 BC
3	Ashoka	274 BC - 232 BC
4	Dasaratha	232 BC - 224 BC
5	Samprati	224 BC - 215 BC
6	Salisuka	215 BC - 202 BC
7	Devavarman	202 BC - 195 BC
8	Satadhanvan	195 BC - 187 BC
9	Brihadatha	187 BC - 185 BC

Sunga Dynasty (185 to 73 B.C.)

- Pushyamitra Sunga was the senapati of last king of Mauryan empire Brihadratha. He killed Brihadratha and founded the Sunga dynasty in 187 B.C.
- Its capital was Pataliputra but later Vidhisha was the capital of Sunga rulers.

Kanva Dynasty (73-28 B.C.)

- Founder- Vasudeva Kanva.
- Other Sunga Rulers: Bhumimitra, Narayana, Susarman.

Satvahana Dynasty

- It ruled in the Deccan and Central India after Mauryans.
- Founder- Simuka
- Most powerful Satavahana king - Gautamiputra Satakarni (A.D. 106-130)

Other Dynasties

- **Kharavela** was the greatest king of Chedi Dynasty.
- Source of information: **Hatigumpha** Pillar inscription (Created by Kharavela)
- The **Sakas** were a group of nomadic tribes of Iranian origin or Scythian tribes, who lived in Central Asia.
- **Kanishka** is considered to have conflicted with the Pataliputra and had taken Asvaghosa, the Buddhist Monk to Purushpura.
- Founder of **Pallava** Dynasty- **Simhavishnu**, Capital – **Kanchi**.

The Sangam Kingdom

The Tamil Sangam was an academy of poets and bards.

Sangam	Place of Organisation	Chairman	Kingdom
First	Thenmadurai	Agastya	Pandiya
Second	Kapatapuram	Earlier- Agastya Later- Tolkappiyar (a disciple of Agastaya)	Pandiya
Third	North Madurai	Nakkirar	Pandiya

- Founder of **Chera Dynasty**: Utiyan Cheralatan.
- Founder of **Chola Dynasty**: Vijayalaya Capital – **Kaveripattanam.**

Temples & their location

The Kailash Temple	Ellora
The Hoysala temple	Belur and Halebid
The Chennakesava temple	Belur
The Hoysaleswara temple	Halebid
The Ratha and Shore temple	Mahabalipuram,
The Brihadeshwara temple	Tanjavur
The Vithala temple	Harmpi
The Meenakshi Temple	Madurai

The Gupta Empire (AD 320-467)

- Founder - Sri Gupta
- **Nalanda University** was built by Kumargupt.
- The great Mathematician **Aryabhata lived** during this age. He discovered the number "0" and value of **Pi.** He wrote "**Aryabhatiya**" and "Suryasiddhanta".
- **Kalidas** the great poet also belonged to this period.
- **Chandragupta (320-335 AD)** was the son of Ghatotkacha and grandson of Sri Gupta.
- **Sumudragupta** (AD 335-375) Harisena described him as the "Hero of a Hundred Battles."

- **Prayag Prashasti** (Written by **Harisen**) is the main source of information on his reign.
- **Samundragupta** was succeeded by his son Chandragupta Vikramaditya (or II).
- **Kumaragupta (AD 415-455)** is the son of Chandragupta II.
- Gupta Period is also known as the **'Golden Age of Ancient India'.**

The Post Gupta Period (550 AD – 647 AD)

SOUTHERN INDIA

- Capital of **Chalukyas** (AD 543-753)- **Badami** (Bagalkot district of North Karnataka)
- **Pulakeshin I** is generally attributed to be the first Chalukyan king.
- Narasimhavarman completed the beautiful temples of **Mahablipuram.**

Rashtrakutas (AD 753–973)

- Founded by **Dantidurg**; Krishna I built **Kailasha** temple at **Ellora**. Amoghavarsha, who is compared to Vikramaditya, wrote the first Kannada poetry Kaviraj Marg.

Gangas

Ruled Orissa; Narsimhadeva constructed **Sun Temple** at Konark; Anantvarman built the **Jagannath Temple** at Puri; and Kesaris who used to rule before Gangas built the **Lingaraja Temple** at Bhubaneshwar.

Pushyabhuti Dynasty (600-647 A.D.)

- The greatest king was **Harshavardhana**, son of Prabhakar Vardhana of Thaneshwar. He shifted the capital to **Kannauj.**
- **Hieun Tsang** visited during his reign.
- Harsha himself wrote three plays – Priyadarhika, Ratnawali and Nagananda.

Pallavas (AD 600-757)

Founder-**Simhavishnu**; capital-**Kanchi**; greatest king **Narsimhavarman** who founded the town of Mamallapuram (**Mahabalipuram**).

- **Palas** dynasty was founded by Gopala I, who was elected as king of people.
- **Palas** with capital at **Monghyr** is known for Dharmapala, their second king, who founded **Vikramashila University** and revived Nalanda University.
- The greatest ruler of **Pratiharas** was Bhoja (also known as Mihir, Adivraha).

Chalukyas (543-755 A.D.)

- **Pulakesin I** was the founder of the Chalukya dynasty. He established a small kingdom with **Vatapi** or **Badami** as its capital.
- Their cave temples are found in Ajanta, Ellora and Nasik.

The Cholas (AD 985-1279)

- Founder **Vijayalaya**, Capital **Tanjore**.
- **Aditya I** Chola wiped out Pallavas and weakened Pandayas.
- **Purantaka I** captured Madurai, but defeated by Rashtrakuta ruler Krishna III at the **Battle of Takkolam.**

Ancient Indian Books and Authors

Buddhacharita	- Asvaghosha
Kirtarjuniya	- Bharavi
Ravanavadha	- Bhatti
Ratnavali	- Harshavardhana
Priyadarshika	- Harshavardhana
Uttar Ramacharita	- Bhavabhuti
Brihat Katha Manjari	- Kshemendra
Katha Sarita Sagara	- Somadeva
Charak Samhita	- Charak

MODERN HISTORY

Early Medieval Period

Tripartite Struggle

- Tripartite conflict was fought among the Gurjara-Pratiharas, Rashtrkutas and Palas for the control over Kannauj.

The Rajputs

- The period between 647 A.D. and 1192 A.D., i.e. 500 years is known as the Rajput period in the history of India.
- The most powerful Rajputs: **Gahadavalas** (Kanauj), the **Paramaras**(Malwa), and the Chauhans (Ajmer).
- **Prithviraj Chauhan's** (1178-92 AD) empire included Punjab, Haryana, Rajasthan and Uttar Pradesh.
- His court's poet **Chand Bardai** wrote Prithviraj Chauhan's biography "**Prithviraj Raso**".
- He defeated **Shahabuddin Muhammad Ghori** in the first battle of **Tarrain** in **1191.**

- In the **Second battle of Tarrain** (1192) Muhammad Ghori won and killed Prithviraj Chauhan.
- **Jayachandra** was the king of Kannauj. Muhammad Ghori defeated and killed Jayachandra in the Battle of Chadawar in 1194.
- Rana Kumbha was the ruler of Mewar, a state in western India.
- **Dilwara temples** at **Mount Abu**, the Vimala Vasahi and the Luna Vasahi were built by Solankis of Gujarat.

Medieval India

The Delhi Sultanate (1206 – 1526 AD)

Dynasties of Delhi Sultanate

(i)	Slave Dynasty	:	1206-1290 AD
(ii)	Khilje	"	1290-1320 AD
(iii)	Tughlaq	"	1320-1414 AD
(iv)	Sayyid	"	1414-1451 AD
(v)	Lodhi	"	1451-1526 AD

- **Sources of Medieval Indian History**: Tarikh i Firoze Shahi (Ziauddin barani); Tuzuk-i-Mubarak Shahi (Yahaya bin Ahmed Sirhindi); Futuhat-i-Firoze Shahi (Firoze Shah Tughluq), etc.
- **Muhammad Ghori** nominated his trusted and prominent **slave, Qutubuddin Aibak** as his representative to govern the newly conquered regions in India. It was the beginning of slave dynasty.

The Mamluk dynasty or The Slave Dynasty (1206-1290 AD)

- **Qutubuddin Aibak** also began the construction of **Qutub Minar**, in the honour of famous Sufi Saint **Khwaja Qutubuddin Bakhityar Kaki.**
- **Shamsuddin Iltutmish** was a slave of Qutubuddin Aibak.
- **Iltutmish** stopped the Mongol attack in 1221 A.D led by **Chenghiz Khan.**
- Iltutmish nominated **his daughter Razia** as the successor.
- She was the first and only Muslim lady that ever ruled in India.
- She further offended the nobles by her preference for an **Abyssian slave Yakut.**
- In 1240 A.D, **Razia** was the victim of a conspiracy and was killed near **Kaithal** (Haryana).

- **Jalaluddin Khilji** founded Khilji dynasty.
- **Alauddin Khilji** was the nephew and son-in-law of Jalaluddin Khilji.
- He killed Jalaluddin Khilji and took over the throne in 1296.
- He was the first **Turkish Sultan of Delhi** who **separated religion from politics**.
- He appointed **Diwan-i-Riyasat** and **Shahna-i-Mandi** to regulate the fixed price market.
- He abolished **Iqtas** of royal troopers and the payment of their salaries in cash.
- He constructed monuments like **Alai-Darwaza** and **Sirifort** in Delhi.
- **Ghazi Malik** with the name of Ghiyasuddin Tughluq became the Sultan of Delhi in 1320.
- **Mohammad-bin-Tughlaq** organised better **postal system.**
- **Ghiyasuddin Tughlaq** ascended the throne in 1325.
- **Firoz Shah Tughlaq** established Diwan-i-Khairat (department for poor and needy people), and Diwan-l-Bundagan (department of slaves).
- **Khizr Khan** was the first Sultan of the **Sayyed Dynasty.**
- The other rulers of this dynasty were Mubarak Shah (1421-1434), Muhammad Shah (1434-1443), Alam Shah (1443-1451).
- **Bahlol Lodhi** (1451-88 A.D.) was an **Afghan Sardar** who founded the Lodhi dynasty.
- **Sikandar Lodhi** shifted his capital from Delhi to Agra and conquered Bihar and Western Bengal.
- **Ibrahim Lodhi** was the last king of Lodhi dynasty and the last Sultan of Delhi.
- At last **Daulat Khan Lodhi**, the governor of Punjab invited Babur to overthrow Ibrahim Lodhi, Babur accepted the offer and inflicted a crushing defeat on Ibrahim Lodhi in the **first battle of Panipat** in 1526.

Vijaynagar Empire (1336-1565 AD)

- The **Vijayanagar Empire** was a South Indian dynasty based in the **Deccan** on the South bank of **Tungabhadra** River.
- There were four dynasties ruled over Vijaynagar —Sangama Dynasty, Saluva Dynasty, Tuluva Dynasty and Aravidu Dynasty.

Bahmani Kingdom

- The Bahmani Kingdom of Deccan's capital was **Gulbarga**.
- It was founded by Hasan Gangu (original name–Ismail Mukh).
- He took the tittle of Alauddin Hasan, Bahaman Shah.

Religious Movements

Bhakti Movement

- **Bhakti** means personal devotion to God. It stresses the Union of the individual with God.
- **Bhakti movement** originated in South India between the 7th and the 12th centuries AD.
- **Ramananda** was disciple of Ramunaja. He was the first reformer to preach in Hindi.
- **Kabir** was an ardent disciple of Ramananda. He wanted unity between the Hindus and the Muslims.
- **Namdeva** was a waterman by birth. He composed beautiful hymns in Marathi.
- **Nanak** was the founder of the Sikh religion.
- Nanak's teachings were in the form of verses. They were collected in a book called the **Adi Granth**.
- Later Adi Grantham was written in a script called **Gurmukhi**.
- **Chaitaniya**, a great devotee of Lord Krishna, was a saint from Bengal.
- **Tulsidas** composed the famous **Ramcharitamanas** in Hindi, expounding the various aspects of Hindu dharma.
- **Surdas** was a devotee of Lord Krishna and Radha. His works include **Sursagar**, **Sahitya Ratna** and Sur Sarawali.
- **Dadu Dayal** was a disciple of Kabir. His followers were known as Dadu Panthis.
- **Eknath** was a devotee of Vithoba. He wrote commentary on verses of the Bhagavad Gita.

The Sufi Movement

- **Sufism** is basically a religion based on the truth of life. The **mystics of Islam** are called **Sufis**.
- It emerged in India in 11th & 12th century A.D.
- It established brotherhood between Hindus & Muslims.
- The founders of the most important Sufi lineage Chisti, Suhrawardi, Qadiri, Naqshbandi originally came from central and west Asia.
- The prominent sufi saints were Khwaja Nizamuddin Aulia, Ganj-e-Shakar Fariduddin, Qutubuddin Bakhtiyar Kaki and Hamuddin Nagori .
- **Hazrat Nizam-ud-Din** was the disciple of Fariduddin Ganj-i-Shakkar.
- **Qutbuddin Bakhtiar Kaki** was the disciple and the spiritual successor of Moinuddin Chishti.

Khwaja Moinuddin Chishti (1142-1236 AD)

- The Chisti order of Sufism was founded in **village Khwaja** Chishti near **Herat** in Persia, i.e. Iran.
- In India, Chisti silsila was founded by Khwaja Moinuddin Chishti (born 1142 AD).
- He came to India around AD 1192.
- He made **Ajmer** the main centre for his teachings. He died in Ajmer in 1236.

The Mughals (1526-1540 and 1555-1857)

- The **Mughul era** began with the Babur's victory over Ibrahim Lodi in the First Battle Of Panipat in 1526.'
- **Babur** was from the princely **family of mixed Mongol and Turkish blood**.
- He died in 1530.
- **Humayun** succeeded Babur at the young age of 23 in 1530.
- He was defeated in the Battle of Chausa (1539) and Battle of Kanauj (1540) by **Sher Shah Suri** who became the ruler of Agra and Delhi.
- The Humayun's Tomb was built by his widow Haji Begum in Delhi.
- Humayun's sister **Gulbadan Begum** wrote **Humayunnama**.
- He died in 1556.
- The real name of **Sher Shah** was **Farid**.
- During the siege of the fort of **Kalinjar** one of the cannons accidentally went off killing him on 26th of May 1535.
- He was buried in **Sasaram** (Dihar).
- He built **Purana Qila** in Delhi.
- **Bairam Khan** became the Wakil of the kingdom with the title of Khan-i-Khana.
- **Akbar** was crowned at **Kalanaur** at the age of 13 years in 1556.
- Akbar reoccupied Delhi and Agra in the second battle of Panipat with Hemu, a general of Adil Shah in 1556.

- **Akbar** built many buildings like **Agra Fort** (1565), **Lahore Palace** (1572), Fatehpur Sikri, Buland Darwaza and Allahabad Fort (1583).
- He died in 1605.

Nine Jewels or Nav-Ratnas of Akbar
Abdul Rahim – Hindi Scholar
Abdul Fazal – Chief Advisor
Birbal – Wittiness
Tansen – Singer
Todar Mal – Finance Minister
Mullah Do Piaza – Advisor
Raja Man Singh – General (Senapati)
Faizi – Poet
Hamim Humam – Physician

Jahangir (AD 1605-1627)

- The real name of **Jahangir** was **Salim**.
- Jahangir married **Mehr-un-Nisa** who assumed the title of **'Nur Jahan'** (Light of the world)
- His son **Khurram** (Shah Jahan) rebelled against him at the end of his reign.
- **Shah Jahan** became emperor in 1627.
- He was married to the daughter of **Asaf Khan** named **Arjumand Bano Begum,** also known as **Mumtaz Mahal.**
- He built the **Taj Mahal** in Agra and the Jama Masjid (sand stone) in Delhi.

Auranzeb (AD 1658-1707)

- **Aurangzeb** was also called as **Zinda Pir** (the living saint).
- The **Mughul** conquest reached a climax during his reign.
- The second coronation of Aurangzeb took place when he defeated Dara (1659).
- He **forbade inscription of Kalma on the coins** and banned music in the court.
- He died in 1707 AD.

The Later Mughals

- **Muazzam** ascended the Mughal throne with the title of **Bahadur Shah.**
- **Farrukhsiyar** ascended the throne with help of Sayyid brothers, Abdullah Khan and Hussain Khan.
- **Nadir Shah** raided India in 1738-39 and took away the **peacock throne** and **Kohinoor diamond** during the reign of Mohammad Shah (1719-48).
- The **Battle of Buxar** (1764) was fought during the reign of Shah Alam II.
- **Bahadur Shah Zafar** was the last Mughal king.

Name of the Book- Author
Tuzk-i-Babari : Babar
Akbarnama, Aini Akbari : Abul Fazl
TuzkiJahangiri : Jahangir
Shah Jahan Namah : Inayat Khan
Padshah Namah (about Shah Jahan): Abdul Hamid Lahori
Alamgirnama (about Aurangzeb) : Mirza Muhammad Kazim

Battles Fought Between
1st Battle of Panipat (1526) : Babur and Ibrahim Lodhi
Battle of Khanwa (1527) : Babur and Rana Sunga.
Battle of Chausa (1539) : Sher Shah Suri and Humayun
2nd Battle of Panipat (1556) : Akbar and Hemu
Battle of Haldighati (1576) : Raja Maan Singh (Mughal army) and Rana Pratap
Battle of Samugarh (1658) : Aurangzeb and Dara Shikoh
Battle of Khanwa (1659) : Aurangzeb and brother Shah Shuja
Battle of Karnal (1739) : Nadir Shah and Muhammad Shah(Mughal)

Maratha State (1674-1818)

- **Shivaji** was born at Shivner, Poona and died on April 3, 1680 in Rajgarh.
- He was founder of the Maratha kingdom of India.
- **Shahji Bhonsle** was the father and Jija Bai was the mother of Shivaji.
- In 1659, **Shivaji killed Afzal Khan** who was deputed by Adil Shah to suppress him.

Sikh Gurus

- **Nanak** (1469-1539) founded Sikh religion.
- **Angad** (1538-52) invented **Gurmukhi.**
- **Amardas** (1552-74) struggled against **sati system** and **purdah system** and established 22 Gadiyans to propagate religion.
- **Ramdas** (1574-81) founded Amritsar in 1577. Akbar granted the land.
- **Arjun** (1581-1606) founded **Swarn Mandir** (Golden Temple) and composed Adi Granth.
- **Hargobind Singh** (1606-45) established **Akal Takht** and fortified Amritsar.
- **Har Rai** (l 645-66)
- **Harkishan** (1661-64)
- **Tegh Bahadur** (1664-75)
- **Gobind Singh** (1675-1708) was the last Guru who founded the **Khalsa.** After him Sikh guruship ended.

MODERN HISTORY

Arrival of Europeans in India

Portuguese

- On 17th May 1498, **Vasco da Gama**, a Portuguese navigator, came to **Calicut**.
- He found new trade route from Europe to Asia via **Cape of Good Hope**.
- His second visit in 1502 established Portuguese Trading Centres at Calicut, Cannanore and Cochin.
- **Cochin** was the first capital of the Portuguese in India which was shifted to Goa later on.

Dutch

- Dutch arrived in India as a beginning of Portuguese decline in 1605.
- The Dutch East India company of Netherlands was formed in 1592 to trade with East Indies.
- **Cornelis Houtman** was the first Dutch who came to India.

French

- In AD 1664 French came to India as a last European Community.
- The French East India Company was founded by **Jean Baptiste Colbert.**
- In 1667, the first French Factory was established at Surat.

Danes

- In 1616 the Danes came to India.
- They established at **Tranquebar (Tamil Nadu)** in 1620 and Serampore (Bengal) in 1676.

East India Company

- **Company rule** in India effectively began in 1757 after the **Battle of Plassey.**
- Company was granted the diwani, or the right to collect revenue, in Bengal and Bihar in 1765.
- **Siraj-ud-Daula** was the last independent Nawab of Bengal who succeeded Alivardi Khan to the throne.
- **Mir Jafar Ali Khan Bahadur**, commonly known as Mir Jafar, (c. 1691–February 5, 1765) was the **first Nawab of Bengal under Company rule** in India.

- After Siraj decline Mir Jafar was installed as the Nawab in 1757 by the British East India Company.
- **Mir Qasim** (May 8, 1777) was the Nawab of Bengal from 1760 to 1763.
- The **Battle of Buxar** was fought on 23 October **1764** between East India Company led by **Hector Munro** and the combined army of **Mir Qasim**, the Nawab of Bengal: the **Nawab of Awadh** and the **Mughal King Shah Alam II.**

Rule of the British Governer and Governor Generals

- After the victory of the English in Buxar, Clive was appointed the governor and **commander-in-chief** of the English possessions in Bengal.
- **Warren Hastings** was appointed the Governor of Bengal in 1772.
- In 1773 **the Regulating Act** was passed which provided for the setting up of a supreme court to try all British subjects.
- **Lord Wellesley** is considered to be one of the most brilliant Governor Generals of Bengal.
- He **introduced the Subsidiary Alliance system** to undo with the French influence and bring the Indian states within the purview of the British power of Jurisdiction.
- **Lord Minto-I (AD 1807-13)** was followed by Lord Hastings who governed from 1813 to 1823.
- **Marquess of Hastings (AD 1813-1823)–** He was the first to appoint Indians to the highest posts of responsibility. The **first vernacular newspaper Samachar Patrika** published during his time.
- **Lord William Bentinck (AD 1828-35)–** Charter Act of 1833 was passed and he was made the first Governor General of India; Abolition of sati in 1829.
- **Lord Dalhousie (AD 1848-56)– Doctrine of Lapse**, The Second Burmese war, The Second Anglo Sikh War, Shimla made the summer capital, **First railway line was laid from Bombay to Thane, in 1853.**
- **Lord Canning (AD 1856-58)** - Annexation of Avadh, enactment of Hindu Widow Remarriage Bill, 1857, **establishment of**

universities at Calcutta, Madras and Bombay, revolt of 1857.

➢ Following the Queen's recommendation in 1858, transferring the Government from the company to the British Crown, **Lord Canning** was made the **first Viceroy** of India.

• **Lord Mayo (AD 1869-72)–** Organised **first census** which was held **in 1871.**

• **Lord Lytton (AD 1876-80)–** The Delhi Durbar, January 1, 1877 and the Ve**rnacular Press Act,** 1878.

• **Lord Ripon (AD 1880-84)** – First Factory Act of 1881. **Local Self-Government was introduced in 1882.** Repeat of Vernacular Press act.

• **Lord Curzon (AD 1899-1905)** - Famine Commission, Agriculture Research Institute at Pusa, **Partition of Bengal** in 1905.

• **Lord Minto II (AD 1905-10)–** Minto-Morley Reforms in 1909. Swadeshi movement (1905-08), foundation of Muslim League (1906), Surat session and split in the congress (1907).

➢ **Capital of country was announced to be shifted from Calcutta to Delhi.**

• **Lord Chelmsford (1916-21)–** Government of India Act 1919 (Montague-Chelmsford Reforms), enactment of Rowlatt Act (1919), **Jallianwala Bagh Tragedy (1919),** beginning of the Non-co-operation Movement.

• **Lord Irwin (AD 1926-31)–** Appointment of **Simon commission** in 1928. Gandhi-Irwin Pact in 1931; First Around Table Conference (1930).

• **Lord Willington (AD 1931-36)–** The Second Round Table Conference 1931, The communal award, 1932, the Poona pact, Third Round Table Conference, 1932.

• **Lord Wavell (AD 1944-47)-** Wavell Plan and Shimla Conference, Cabinet Mission (Lawrence, Cripps and Alexander), Direct Action Day" on August 16, 1946, Attlee's Declaration,

• **Lord Mountbatten, (March 1947-June 1948) Last Viceroy of British India** and first-Governor general of free India. Partition of India in third week of June, 1947; Indian Independence Act, Partition of the country between two independent states of India and Pakistan. He was **succeeded by C. Rajagopalachari.**

Some Important rulers in India (1720-1949)

Ruler	Period	Place
1. Sadat Khan Burhan-ul-Mulk	1722-39	Awadh
2. Safdar Jung	1739-54	Awadh
3. Shuja-ud-daulah	1754-75	Awadh
4. Asaf-ud-daulah	1775-97	Awadh
5. Wazir Ali	1797-98	Awadh
6. Nizam-ul-Mulk Asaf Jah	1724-48	Hyderabad
7. Nasir Jung	1748-50	Hyderabad
8. Muzaffar Jung	1750-51	Hyderabad
9. Salabat Jung	1751-60	Hyderabad
10. Nizam Ali	1760-1803	Hyderabad
11. Sikandar Jah	1803-29	Hyderabad
12. Nasir-ud-daulah	1829-57	Hyderabad
13. Afjal-ud-daulah	1857-69	Hyderabad
14. Mahabat Ali Khan	1869-1911	Hyderabad
15. Osman Ali Khan	1911-49	Hyderabad
16. Hyder Ali	1761-82	Mysore
17. Tipu Sultan	1782-99	Mysore
18. Ranjit Singh	1792-1839	Punjab

The Revolt of 1857

• **Political Causes:** The policy of Doctrine of Lapse.

• **Nana Sahib** was refused pension, as he was the adopted son of Peshwa Baji Rao I.

• **Military Discrimination:** Discrimination between the Indian and the British soldiers.

• **Religious Discrimination:** The introduction of Enfield rifle, the cartridge of which was greased with animal fat, provided the spark.

• On March 29, 1857, a soldier named **Mangal Pandey** attacked and fired at his senior at Barrackpur in Bengal (in 19th and 34th Native infantry).

• Mutiny spread throughout UP along with some other parts of the country.

• **Mughal emperor Bahadur Shah II** was proclaimed the Emperor of India.

• **Causes of Failure of the Revolt:** Lack of planning, organization and leadership.

• Some Indians supported the British in suppressing the revolt as **Scindia of Gwalior, the Holkar of Indore, the Nizam of Hyderabad, the Raja of Jodhpur, the Nawab of Bhopal, the rulers of Patiala, Sindh and Kashmir and the Rana of Nepal.**

Social and Cultural Reforms

• **Raja Rammohan Roy** established the **Brahmo Samaj** at Calcutta in 1828 in order to purify Hinduism and to preach **monotheism.**

- Raja Rammohan Roy is most remembered for helping Lord William Bentinck to declare the **practice of Sati** a punishable offence in **1829**.
- **Henry Vivian Derozio** was the founder of the Young Bengal Movement.
- The original name of **Swami Vivekananda** was Narendranath Dutta (1863-1902).
- He was famous disciple of Shri **Ramkrishna Paramahamsa**.
- Swami Vivekananda participated at the Parliament of Religions held in Chicago (USA) on **September 11,1893** and raised the prestige of India and Hinduism very high.
- The **Theosophical Society** was founded in New York (USA) in 1875 by **Madam H.P. Blavatsky,** a Russian lady, and **Henry Steel Olcott,** an American colonel.
- The **Aligarh Movement** was started by **Sir Syed Ahmad Khan** (1817-98) for the social and educational advancement of the Muslims in India.

SOME IMPORTANT ORGANIZATION

Name of the Organization	Founder	Year	Place
Atmiya Sabha	Ram Mohan Roy	1815	Calcutta
Brahmo Samaj	Ram Mohan Roy	1828	Calcutta
Dharma Sabha	Radhakanta Dev	1829	Calcutta
Tattvabodhini Sabha	Debendranath Tagore	1839	Calcutta
Nirankaris	Dayal Das, Darbara Singh, Rattan Chand etc.	1840	Punjab
Manav Dharma Sabha	Durgaram Manchharam	1844	Surat
Parmahansa Mandali	Dadoba Panderung	1849	Bombay
Namdharis	Ram Singh	1857	Punjab
Radha Swami Satsang	Tulsi Ram	1861	Agra
Brahom Samaj of India	Keshab Chandra Sen	1866	Calcutta
Dar-ul-Ulum	Maulana Hussain Ahmed	1866	Deoband
Prarthna Samaj	Dr. Atmaram Pandurung	1867	Bombay
Arya Samaj	Swami Dayanand Saraswati	1875	Bombay
Sudharam Brahmo Samaj	Anand Mohan Bose	1878	Calcutta
Deccan Education Society	G. G. Agarkar	1884	Pune (Poona)
Muhammadan Educational Conference	Sir Syed Ahmad Khan	1886	Aligarh
Indian National Conference	M. G. Ranade	1887	Bombay
Deva Samaj	Shivnarayan Agnihotri	1887	Lahore
Nadwah-ul-Ulma	Maulana Shibli Numani	1894	Lucknow
Ramakrishna Mission	Swami Vivekanand	1897	Belur
Servants of Indian Society	Gopalakrishan Gokhale	1905	Bombay
Poona Seva Sadan	Mrs Ramabai Ranade and G.K. Devadhar	1909	Pune (Poona)
Social Service League	N. M. Joshi	1911	Bombay
Seva Samiti	H. N. Kunzru	1914	Allahabad

The Freedom Struggle

- The **Indian National Congress** was founded on 28 December 1885 by Allan Octavian Hume.
- **Womesh Chandra (W.C.) Bonnerjee** was the **first President of the INC.**
- The **first session of the INC was** held **from 28–31 December 1885, and was attended by 72 delegates.**
- Bengal was reunited in 1911.
- **Surat Split** is mainly known for separation of Congress partymen into moderates and extremists at the Surat session of Congress in 26 December 1907.
- The **All-India Muslim League** was founded on 30 December **1906.**
- The founding president of **Ghadar Party** was Sohan Singh Bhakna and Lala Hardayal was the co-founder of this party.
- In 1916, two **Home Rule Movements** were launched in the country: one under the leadership of Bal Gangadhar Tilak and the other under Annie Besant.
- **August Declaration (1917)**
  The British aimed at "increasing association of Indians in every branch of the administration for progressive realisation of responsible government in India as an integral part of the British empire".
- On February 5, 1922, in the **Chauri Chaura** the police chowki was set on fire by the mob, killing 22 of the police occupants.

- The **Lahore protest** was led by Indian nationalist Lala Lajpat Rai, was severely beaten by local police. He died on November 17, 1928.

> **First Round Table Conference** (November 1930 – January 1931).
> **Second Round Table Conference** (September – December 1931)
> **Third Round Table Conference** (November – December 1932)

- The name "Pakistan" had been proposed by Choudhary Rahmat Ali in his Pakistan Declaration.

  In 1940 at the **Lahore Session** of the Muslim League, the **demand for a separate state of Pakistan was made.**

- It was based on the two-nation theory.
- **Quit India Movement (1942)**

  A.I. Congress Committee passed Quit India Resolution at Bombay on 8 August, 1942.

- Gandhiji gave the slogan "**Do or Die**" on 8 Aug, 1942.
- The **Indian National Army** was an armed force formed by Indian nationalists in 1942 in Southeast Asia during World War II.
- Cabinet Mission (1946) was composed of three Cabinet Ministers of England: **Sir Pethick Lawrence, Sir Stafford Cripps,** and **Alexander.**

Newspapers and Journals

Newspaper/Journal Name	Founder
Bengal Gazette (1780) (India's First Newspaper)	James Augustus Hickey.
Kesari	B.G.Tilak
Amrita Bazar Patrika	Sisir Kumar Ghosh and Motilal Ghosh
Hindu	Vir Raghavacharya and G.S. Aiyar
Hindustan	M.M. Malviya
Mooknayak	B.R. Ambedkar
Comrade	Mohammad Ali
Tahzib-ul-Akhlaq	Sir Syed Ahmed Khan
Al-Hilal	Abul Kalam Azad
Independent	Motilal Nehru
Punjabi	Lala Lajpat Rai
New India (Daily)	Annie Besant

Pratap	Ganesh Shankar Vidyarthi
Young India	M.K Ghandhi
Hindustan Times	K.M. Pannikar

Sayings of Important Persons

1.	'Do or Die'	Mahatma Gandhi (while launching Quit India movement in 1942)
2.	'Give me blood and I will give you freedom'	Subhash Chandra Bose (in his address to soldiers of Azad Hind Fauj)
3.	'Dilli Chalo'	Subhash Chandra Bose's battle cry of Azad Hind Fauj
4.	'My ultimate aim is to wipe every tear from every eye'	Jawaharlal Nehru
5.	'Jai Jawan, Jai Kisan'	Lal Bahadur Shastri
6.	'Saare Jahan Se Achcha, Hindustan Hamara'	Dr. Mohammed Iqbal
7.	'Sarfaroshiki tamanna Ab Hamare Dil mein Hai'	Ram Prasad Bismill
8.	'Swaraj is my birthright and I will have it'	Bal Gangadhar Tilak
9.	'Inqualab Zindabad'	Bhagat Singh
10.	'Vande Mataram'	Bankim Chandra Chatterjee
11.	'Hindi, Hindu, Hindustan'	Bhartendu Harishchandra
12.	Back to Vedasi	Dayanand Saraswati

Books & Authors of Modern India

1.	Ghulam Giri	Jyotiba Phule
2.	Causes of the Indian Mutiny	Sir Syed Ahmed Khan
3.	The Discovery of India	J.L. Nehru
4.	Unhappy India	Lala Lajpat Rai
5.	Anandmath	Bankim chand Chatterjee
6.	What Congress and Gandhi have done to the untouchables	Dr. B.R. Ambedkar
7.	Satyarth Prakash	Swami Dayanand
8.	India Divided	Dr. Rajendra Prasad
9.	Neel Darpan	Dinbandhu Mitra
10.	Hind Swaraj	M.K. Gandhi

Polity

The Preamble

- The Preamble to Indian Constitution is **based on "Objective Resolution"** of Nehru. Jawaharlal Nehru introduced an objective resolution on December 13, 1946 and it was adopted by Constituent Assembly on 22 January, 1947.
- Initially, the Preamble was drafted by **Sh. B. N. Rau** in his memorandum of May 30, 1947 and was later reproduced in the Draft of October 7, 1947.

The Preamble Reads

"WE, THE PEOPLE OF INDIA, having solemnly resolved to constitute India into a SOVEREIGN, SOCIALIST, SECULAR, DEMOCRATIC, REPUBLIC and to secure to all its citizen:

JUSTICE, social, economic and political;

LIBERTY of thought, expression, belief, faith and worship;

EQUALITY of status and of opportunity; and to promote among them all

FRATERNITY assuring the dignity of the individual and the unity and integrity of the nation:

IN OUR CONSTITUENT ASSEMBLY, this 26th day of November 1949, do hereby ADOPT, ENACT and GIVE TO OURSELVES THIS CONSTITUTION.

Constitution of India

- **Originally** our Constitution contained **395 Articles divided in 22 Parts and 8 Schedules.**
- The Constitution, in **its current form,** consists of **a Preamble, 24 Parts containing 448 articles, 12 schedules.**
- **India is a union of 29 States and 7 Union Territories.**
- It lays down Directive Principles of State Policy for the guidance of Legislature and the Executive of the country.
- It establishes independence of judiciary from the executive.

The Union & Its Territory

- **Article 1** stipulates that **India, that is Bharat, shall be Union of states.**

- The country is described as **'Union'** because it is **indestructible**.
- Under Articles 2 & 3, Parliament has the power to establish new States, form a new State.
- **First Linguistic State** – Andhra Pradesh.
- States Reorganisation Act 1956 was adopted by the Govt. of India that resulted in the formation of new states & UTs.

Sources of Indian Constitution

Indian Constitution has borrowed its provisions from following sources.

Country	Provisions Borrowed
Government of India Act, 1935	Federal scheme Declaration of emergency powers Ordinance defining the power of the President and Governors Office of the Governor Power of federal judiciary Administration at the centre and state level
United Kingdom	Parliamentary system Bicameral parliament Prime Minister Council of Ministers Single citizenship Office of CAG Writ jurisdiction of courts Rule of law
USA	Written constitution Fundamental rights Supreme Court President as executive head of the state Impeachment of the president, removal of SC and HC judges Vice President as chairman of Rajya Sabha Judicial review, independence of judiciary
Australia	Concurrent list Cooperative federalism Centre State relationship Joint sitting of two houses of Parliament
USSR	Fundamental duties

Country	Provisions Borrowed
Weimer Constitution of Germany	Suspension of fundamental rights during emergency Ballot system
Canada	Federal system Residuary powers Appointment of Governor Advisory jurisdiction of S.C.
South Africa	Procedure of Constitutional amendment. Electing member to Rajya Sabha
Ireland	Concept of Directive Principles of State Policy. Nomination of members to Rajya Sabha by the President. Presidential election.

Directive Principles of State Policy

PART IV Article (36 – 51):

- These Principles are in the nature of instruments of instruction and guidelines to the govt.
- Directives are not enforceable in the Courts and do not create any justiciable rights in favour of the individuals.
- In case of a conflict between Directive Principles and Fundamental Rights of the Constitution, the latter shall prevail.

Fundamental duties

Part IV-A–Article 51-A, added by 42nd Amendment, 1976

It says that it shall be the duty of every citizen of India (there are **eleven such duties**, after the 86th Constitution Amendment Act, 2002):

The Union (Article 51-151)

The President of India

- **Article 52** says that "There shall be a President of India."
- **Article 53** says that the executive power of the Union shall be vested in the President.

Election

The Electoral College consists of:

(a) elected members of both Houses of Parliament, and

(b) elected members of Legislative Assembly of States.

Article 57: The President is eligible for re-Election to that office.

Tenure (Article 56)

The President shall hold office for a **term of 5 years.** The President can resign from his office any time by addressing the **resignation letter to the Vice-President of India**.

Executive Powers - Article 53

All executive powers of the Union are vested in him.

- President appoints the Prime Minister and other ministers; and they hold office during his pleasure.
- He appoints the **Attorney General of India, Comptroller** and **Auditor General of India**, the **Chief Election Commissioner** and other Election Commissioners, the Chairman and Members of the UPSC, the Governors of the states, the Chairman and the members of the Finance Commissions, etc.

The Legislative Powers

- The President can summon or end a session of the Parliament and dissolve the Lok Sabha.

National Emergency

- National emergency is caused by **war, external aggression** or **armed rebellion** in the whole of India or a part of its territory.
- President can declare national emergency only on a written request by the Cabinet Ministers headed by the Prime Minister and the proclamation must be approved by the Parliament within one month.

State Emergency or President's Rule

A State Emergency can be imposed via the following:

1. If that State failed to run Constitutionally, i.e. constitutional machinery has failed - Article 356
2. If that State is not working according to the given direction of the Union Government – Article 365
3. Such an emergency must be approved by the Parliament within a period of two months.

Veto Powers

The President of India is vested with three—absolute veto, suspensive veto and pocket veto.

- **In 1986, President Giani Zail Singh** exercised the pocket veto with respect to the Indian Post Office (Amendment) Bill.

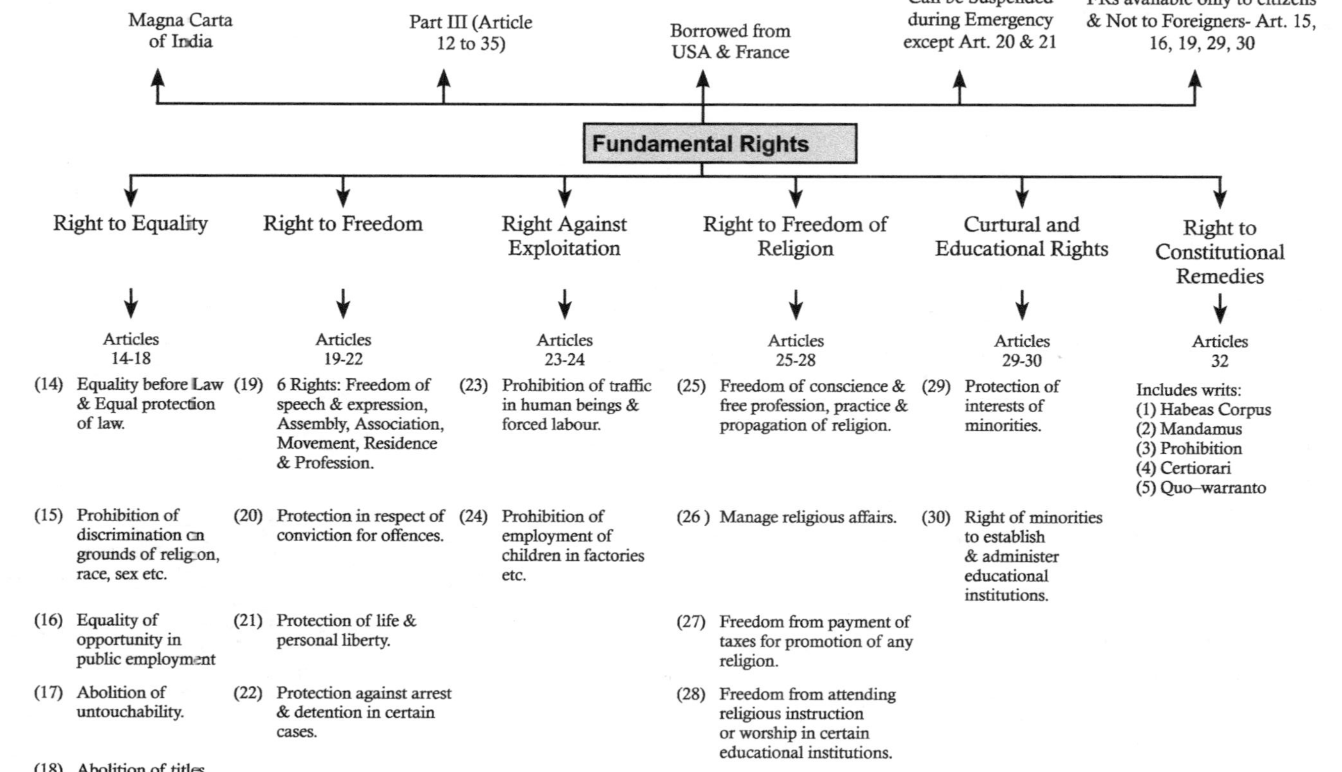

Magna Carta of India

Part III (Article 12 to 35)

Borrowed from USA & France

Can be Suspended during Emergency except Art. 20 & 21

FRs available only to citizens & Not to Foreigners- Art. 15, 16, 19, 29, 30

Fundamental Rights

Right to Equality

Right to Freedom

Right Against Exploitation

Right to Freedom of Religion

Curtural and Educational Rights

Right to Constitutional Remedies

Articles 14-18

Articles 19-22

Articles 23-24

Articles 25-28

Articles 29-30

Articles 32

(14) Equality before Law & Equal protection of law.

(19) 6 Rights: Freedom of speech & expression, Assembly, Association, Movement, Residence & Profession.

(23) Prohibition of traffic in human beings & forced labour.

(25) Freedom of conscience & free profession, practice & propagation of religion.

(29) Protection of interests of minorities.

Includes writs:
(1) Habeas Corpus
(2) Mandamus
(3) Prohibition
(4) Certiorari
(5) Quo–warranto

(15) Prohibition of discrimination on grounds of religion, race, sex etc.

(20) Protection in respect of conviction for offences.

(24) Prohibition of employment of children in factories etc.

(26) Manage religious affairs.

(30) Right of minorities to establish & administer educational institutions.

(16) Equality of opportunity in public employment

(21) Protection of life & personal liberty.

(27) Freedom from payment of taxes for promotion of any religion.

(17) Abolition of untouchability.

(22) Protection against arrest & detention in certain cases.

(28) Freedom from attending religious instruction or worship in certain educational institutions.

(18) Abolition of titles.

The Vice-President (Art. 66-73)

- Article 63 says that there should be a Vice-President of India.
- The Vice-President shall be the ex-officio Chairman of Rajya Sabha (Article 64).
- The Vice-President can be removed from office by a resolution of the Council of States (Rajya Sabha), passed by a majority of its members at that time and agreed to by the House of the People (Lok Sabha). (Article 67)

Council of Ministers

- **Art 74 (1):** It provides that, "There shall be a Council of Ministers with the Prime Minister as its head to aid and advise the President who shall in exercise of his/her functions act in accordance with such advice.
- If the Lok Sabha passes a **'no-confidence motion'**, the entire Council of Ministers including PM has to resign.

The Prime Minister

Prime Minister is the real executive authority.

- **Art 75 (1) :** The Prime Minister shall be appointed by the President and other Ministers shall be appointed by the President on the advice of the Prime Minister.
- He allocates & reshuffles various portfolios among the Ministers.
- Prime Minister is the key link between the Cabinet and the Parliament and keystone of Cabinet architecture.

Union Legislature

- **Part V** of the Constitution deals with Parliament. According to Article 79, there shall be a Parliament for the Union, which shall consists of:
- President of India.
- Two houses consists of Council of States (Rajya Sabha or Upper House) and Lok Sabha or Lower House.

Rajya Sabha (Council of States)

- Its **first sitting was held on April 3, 1952.**
- Article 80 of the Constitution lays down the **maximum strength** of Rajya Sabha as **250,** out of which 12 members are nominated by the President, 238 are representatives of the States and of the two Union Territories.
- The present strength of Rajya Sabha, however, is 245, out of which 233 are representatives of the States and Union Territories of Delhi and Puducherry and 12 are nominated by the President.

- The Rajya Sabha is not subject to dissolution. **The members of the Rajya Sabha are elected for 6 years. One-third of the members retire every two years.**

Lok Sabha (People's House)

- Its **first sitting** took place on **May 13, 1952**
- All the members of the Parliament are popularly elected, except not more than **two** members of the **Anglo-Indian** community, who are nominated by the President.
- **In the Constitution, the strength of the Lok Sabha was provisioned to be not more than 552 : 530 from the States, 20 from the Union Territories and 2 nominated from the Anglo-Indian community.**
- Under the current laws, the strength of Lok Sabha is 545, including the two seats reserved for members of the Anglo-Indian community.

Bills

The bill can broadly be categorised as:
(a) Ordinary bills
(b) Money bills

Ordinary Bills

- All the Bills other than Financial Bills
- Money Bills and the Constitutional Amendment Bills are Ordinary Bills.
- Such Bills can be **introduced in either House of the Parliament** (in Lok Sabha or the Rajya Sabha) **without the recommendation of the President,** except those Bills under Article 3 (i.e., Bills related to reorganisation of the territory of a State).

Money Bills

- Money Bill is defined in Art. 110 of the Constitution.
- As per the Article, any Bill dealing with all or any of the matters enumerated from (a) to (g) of the same Article shall be a Money Bill.
- Money Bills are: imposition, abolition, remission, alteration or regulation of any tax.

Financial Bills

A Financial Bill **cannot be introduced without the President's recommendation, and it can only be introduced in the Lok Sabha.**

Constitutional Amendment Bills

- **Art. 368** deals with the power of the Parliament to amend the Constitution, and the procedure thereof.
- A Bill for this can be introduced in either House (the Lok Sabha or the Rajya Sabha) of the Parliament.

Speaker of the lok sabha

- After formation of a new Lok Sabha the President appoints a **Speaker pro-tem** who is the senior most member of the House.
- A Deputy Speaker is also elected to officiate in the absence of the Speaker.
- **The Speaker is the Chief Presiding Officer of the Lok Sabha.**
- The Speaker and the Deputy Speaker may be **removed from their offices by a resolution passed by the House with an effective majority of the House after a prior notice of 14 days to them.**

The Supreme Court

- The Supreme Court of India is the highest judicial forum and final court of appeal under the Constitution of India with the power of constitutional review.
- **It comprises the Chief Justice of India and 30 other judges.**

Tenure and Qualification and Salary
- Judges of Supreme Court are appointed by the President of India, and service till the age of 65 years.

Impeachment
- A judge of the Supreme Court can be removed under the Constitution only on grounds of proven misconduct or incapacity and by an order of the President of India, after a notice signed by at least 100 members of the Lok Sabha or 50 members of the Rajya Sabha is passed by a two-third majority in each House of the Parliament.

Comptroller and Auditor General (CAG) (Article 148-151)
- **CAG is appointed by the President of India** under Article 148 of the Constitution and shall only be removed from the office in the like manner as a Judge of the Supreme Court.
- The **first CAG of India was V Narahari Rao**

Attorney General of India

- According to Article 76 the Attorney General of India is the Government's chief legal advisor, and its primary lawyer in the Supreme Court of India.

- The First Attorney General was **M.C. Setalvad.**

- **Mukul Rohatgi** is the incumbent Attorney General of India.

The States (Article 152-237)

The Governor (Article 153-162)
- The **Governor of a State is appointed by the President of India** (Article 155).
- The same Governor can act as Governor of more than one State (Article 153-162).

Legislative Assembly (Vidhan Sabha)
- It is the lower and popular house of the State. Members are chosen by direct election
- According to Article 172, duration of Assembly is normally **5 years**. But it may be dissolved earlier by the Governor.

Legislative Council (Article 169)
- It is the upper house.
- Parliament may by law create or abolish Legislative Council.
- It can be created, if the Legislative Assembly of the State passes a resolution to the effect by special majority.

High Courts (Article 214-232)
- There shall be a High Court for each State Article-214.
- The Judiciary in the states consist of a High Court and subordinate courts.
- **There are 24 High Courts in India**
- The **Calcutta High Court** is the **oldest** of all which was established in **1862**. The Bombay and Madras High Courts were established in the same year.
- Chhatisgarh, Uttarakhand (Nainital) and Jharkhand (Ranchi) High Courts were established in the year 2000.

The Panchayati Raj (Article 243-O)
- **Rajasthan is the first state in India,** where Panchayati Raj was implemented in the **73rd Amendment Act, 1992.**
- It gave Constitutional status to Panchayati Raj system.
- After Amendment Panchayati Raj added to the **11th Schedule of the Constitution**

The Three Tire System of Local Governance
- **Gram Panchayat** at Village Level
- **Panchayat Samiti** at Block Level
- **Zila Parishad** at District Level

The Municipalities (Article 243P-243 ZG)
- **PART IX A added by 74th Amendment Act 1992,** gives a constitutional foundation to the local self government units in urban area.
- **Nagar Panchayat**, is for an area being transformed from a rural area to an urban.
- **Municipal Council is for a smaller urban area.**

- **Municipal Corporation is for a larger urban area.** The Municipal Corporation is the topmost urban local government.

Election Commission (Article 324-329)

Article 324 says that the superintendence, direction and control of elections shall be vested in the Election Commission.

Article 325 provides for a single electoral roll for every constituency.

Article 326 stipulates that elections shall be held on the basis of adult suffrage.

Political Parties

- As per the provisions of the Peoples Representation Act, 1951 political parties are registered with the Election Commission of India.
- The **Anti-defection law**, passed in 1985, prevents the MPs or the MLAs elected as candidates from one party forming or joining a new party, unless they comprise more than one-third of the original party, in the Legislature.

Recognition and Reservation of Symbols

- A party registered with the Election Commission may be granted recognition as a National or a State party on the basis of its performance in polls.

Parliamentary Terms

- **Calling Attention:** Moved to call the attention of a Minister to matters of public importance.
- **Interim Government:** This Government is formed during the transitional phase of the history of the country.
- **Ordinance:** An ordinance is a law promulgated by the head of the State in a situation of urgency when the Legislature cannot frame the law because either it is not in session or it is dissolved.
- **Question Hour:** The first one hour period (usually 11: 00 a. m. to 12: 00 a. m.) each day during the meetings of the Parliament is allotted for asking the questions by the members to be replied by the Ministers, is called the Question Hour.
- **Quorum:** It refers to the required presence of the minimum member of members of a body to hold its meetings and conduct its business.
- **Whip:** This is an official appointed by a political party to regulate and monitor the behaviour of its members in the Legislature.
- **Zero Hour:** It is a period which follows after the Question Hour when the members

raise any issue of public importance on very short or even without any notice.

Adjournment motion	• To draw attention of Parliament to a matter of urgent public importance. • Motion needs the support of 50 members for admission. • Rajya Sabha cannot move this motion.
No Confidence Motion	• Moved to prove the confidence of Lok Sabha in the Council of Ministers. • If No Confidence Motion is passed, Council of Ministers has to resign. • No Confidence Motion needs the support of 50 members to be admitted. • Can be moved only in Lok Sabha.

Union Public Service Commission

- The Union Public Service Commission consists of **a Chairman and other** members appointed by the President and they hold office for a **period of 6 years** from the date of their appointment.
- It conducts examinations for appointment to the Services of the Union.
- Age of retirement for a member of **UPSC is 65** years and for a member of **PSC of a State** or a Joint Commission is **62 years.**

NITI Aayog

- NITI Aayog or **National Institution for Transforming India Aayog** is a policy think-tank of Government of India that replaces Planning Commission and aims to involve the States in economic policy-making in India.
- It will be providing strategic and technical advice to the Central and the State Governments. **The Prime Minister heads the Aayog as its chairperson.**

National Development Council(NDC)

- The National Development Council **was formed in 1952,** to associate the States in the formulation of the plans.
- All members of the Union Cabinet, Chief Minister of States, the Administrators of the Union Territories and members of NITI Ayog are members of the NDC.

Finance Commission

- As per **Article 280 of** the Constitution of India the Finance Commission is established.
- It is a **quasi-judicial** body.
- It consists of a chairman and four other members.

Lokpal

In India, the institution of Ombudsman (**Swedish word** meaning **Commissioner**) has given the name of Lokpal & use it as an anti-corruption institution.

Lokayukta

The anti-corruption institution of Lokayukta is set up at the state level. He is appointed by the Governor of the State. In most of the States, the term of office fixed for Lokayukta is **of 5 years duration or 65 years of age,** whichever is earlier.

Advocate General

Each State shall have an Advocate General. He has the **right to address & take part in the proceedings of the House of the State** Legislature. But **he has no right to vote.** His functions are similar to those of the Attorney – General.

How J & K Different from Other States?

Article 370

Under Article 370 of the Indian Constitution, Jammu & Kashmir is granted autonomy. It is a 'temporary provision' that accords special status to the State.

- Directive Principles of State Policy (DPSP) are not applied to J&K but applied to other States.
- President can't declare financial emergency (salaries and allowances reduction, etc.) in relation to J&K.
- High Court of J&K can issue writs only for enforcement of Fundamental Rights.
- Right to property is still guaranteed in J&K.
- Permanent residents of J&K have some special fundamental rights.
- Although Supreme Court, EC and CAG are applicable to J&K along with all other States.

Important Amendments of the Constitution (Article 368)

There are three types of bills that seek to amend the Constitution:

1. Bills that are passed by Parliament by **Simple Majority.**
2. Bills that have to be passed by Parliament by **Special Majority.**
3. Bills that have to be passed by **Special Majority** and also to be **ratified by not less than one-half of the State Legislatures.**

Important Amendments

- **The first Amendment Act** to the Indian Constitution was made in the year 1951. Ninth Schedule was added.
- **The Constitution (24th Amendment) Act, 1971:** It affirmed the power of the Parliament to amend any part of the Constitution.
- **The Constitution (39th Amendment) Act, 1975:** The Act places beyond challenge in courts the election to Parliament of a person holding the office of Prime Minister or Speaker and the election of President and Vice-President.
- **The Constitution (42nd Amendment) Act, 1976:** It was enacted during the period of National Emergency.
- **The Constitution (43rd Amendment) Act, 1978:** It restores civil liberties by deleting Article 3ID which gave powers to Parliament to curtail even legitimate trade union activity under the guise of legislation for the prevention of anti-national activities.
- **The Constitution (44th Amendment) Act, 1978:** Fundamental Rights guaranteed by Articles 20 and 21 cannot be suspended during a national emergency.
- **The Constitution (61st Amendment) Act, 1989:** It lowered the voting age from 21 to 18.
- **The Constitution (73rd Amendment) Act, 1992:** To ensure direct election to all seats in Panchayats.
- **The Constitution (74th Amendment) Act, 1992:** was made to ensure direct election to all seats in Nagarpalikas and Municipalities.
- **102nd Amendment) Act, 2018:** Constitutional status provided to National Commission for Backward Classes (NCBC).
- **The constitution (103rd Amendment) Act, 2019:** 10% Reservation for Economically Weaker Sections (EWS) of the society

Supreme Court Judgments

Case	Judgment
Indian Young Lawyer's Association & Ors. Vs. State of Kerala & Ors.	Supreme court in the Sabarimala case ruled that devotion cannot be subjected to gender discrimination.
Navtej Singh Johar & Ors. Vs. Union of India	Supreme court struck down 157-Year-Old Law which Criminalizes Consensual Homo-Sexual Acts Between Adults. The 5 Judge Bench declared Section 377 IPC unconstitutional, insofar as it criminalises consensual sexual acts of adults in private.
Justice K. S. Puttuswamy (Retd.) and Anr Vs. Union of India & Ors.	Sections 33(2),47& 57 Of Aadhaar Act Struck Down; National Security Exception Gone; Private Entities Cannot Demand Aadhaar Data. Aadhaar is constitutional but making it mandatory for availing government services was unconstitutional. Banks, telecom companies cannot make it mandatory for users to link their Aadhaar with their mobile phones and bank accounts.
Joseph Shine Vs. Union of India	Husband Is Not The Master Of Wife, Adultery Law which criminalizes adultery ruled as unconstitutional, however adultery will be a ground for divorce.
Shayara Bano Vs. Union of India & Ors.	Supreme court ruled that Triple Talaq is unconstitutional
Golaknath Vs. State of Punjab 1967	Supreme Court ruled that Parliament could not restrict any of the Fundamental Rights of individuals enshrined in the Constitution.
Keshavananda Bharti Vs. State of Kerala 1973	Golaknath case was overruled and parliament recaptured the power of amending and by virtue of the amending power cannot change the basic structure of the constitution.
Minerva Mills Vs. Union of India 1980	Fortified the idea of the basic structure which was put forward earlier in the Keshavananda Bharti Case.
Indra Sawhney Vs. Union of India 1992	It defined the "creamy layer" criteria and uphold the execution of the recommendations made by the Mandal Commission
SR Bommai Vs. Union of India 1994	This has created major repercussion on Centre-State relations
Vishaka Vs. State of Rajasthan 1997	Introduction of Vishaka Guidelines and provided basic definitions of sexual harassment at the workplace

Geography

Universe and the Solar System

Universe, the vast and infinite space having million of galaxies is believed to be at least 10 billion light years in diameter it has been expanding since its creation in the Big Bang.

The **Big Bang Theory** is the leading explanation about how the **universe** began.

Solar system consist of 8 planets: Mercury, Venus, Earth, Mars, Jupiter, Saturn, Uranus and Neptune. It also consist of stars.

Planets

Planet	Rolational Time	Orbital Time	No. of Moons
Mercury	59 Days	88 Days	0
Venus	243 Days	255 Days	0
Earth	1 Day	365 Days	1
Mars	1.03 Days	687 Days	2
Jupiter	9 hrs 56 min	11 yrs 11 months	16
Saturn	10 hrs 40 min	29 yrs 5 months	18
Uranus	17 hrs 14 min	84 yrs	17
Neptune	16 hrs 7 min	164 yrs	8
Pluto	6 Days 9 hrs	248 yrs	1

Some facts about planets

1. Biggest Planet is **Jupiter**
2. Biggest Satellite is **Ganymede**
3. Blue Planet is **Earth**
4. Green Planet is **Uranus**
5. Brightest Planet is **Venus**
6. Brightest Planet outside Solar System is **Sirus**
7. Closest Star of Solar System is **Proxima Centauri**
8. Coldest Planet is **Neptune**
9. Evening Star is **Venus**
10. Farthest Planet from Sun is **Neptune**
11. Planet with maximum number of satellites is **Saturn**
12. Fastest revolution in solar system is by **Mercury**
13. Hottest Planet is **Venus**
14. Densest Planet is **Earth**
15. Fastest Rotation in Solar System by **Jupiter**
16. Morning Star is **Venus**
17. Nearest Planet to Earth is **Venus**
18. Nearest Planet to Sun is **Mercury**
19. **Red** Planet is **Mars**
20. Slowest Revolution in Solar System is by **Neptune**
21. Slowest Rotation in Solar System is by **Venus**
22. Smallest Planet is **Mercury**
23. Smallest Satellite is **Deimos**
24. Earth's Twin-is **Venus**
25. Atmosphere like Earth is on **Titan**

Keywords in Universe

- **Constellation :** A group of stars forming some recognised shape.
- **Saptarishi Mandal :** The constellation of Great Bear or Ursa Major.
- **Ursa Major :** One of the most prominent and largest northern constellation also called the Great Bear.
- **Galaxy :** A system of millions or billions of stars found in clusters.
- **Milky Way Galaxy :** Our solar system belongs to this galaxy.
- **Orbits :** The elongated path on which the planets revolve round the sun.
- **Planets :** The bodies made up of rocks or gases and liquids with no light of their own going round the sun.
- **Moon :** Refers to the earth's Moon. Generally all satellites going round their respective planets are also termed as the moons.
- **Asteroids :** Planetoids found located in a gap between Mars and Jupiter.
- **Shooting stars :** The rapidly moving meteors that burn upon entering the earth's atmosphere.
- **Meteorites :** The fragments of meteors falling on the ground or in the oceans.
- **Comets :** A mass of ice and dust with a long tail moving around the solar system.

Earth

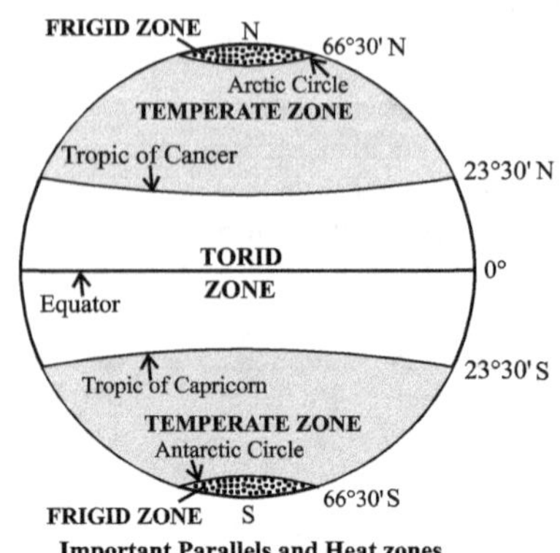

Important Parallels and Heat zones

Facts about Latitude

Lattitudes	Major Continents	Major Countries
Tropic of Cancer	North America, Africa and Asia	Bahamas, Mexico, Mauritania, Mali, Western Sahara, Algeria, Niger, Libya, Egypt, Saudi Arabia, India, China, Abudhabi, Oman, Bangladesh, Burma, and Taiwan.
Equator	South America, Africa, Asia	Equador, Colombia Brazil, Sao Tome & Prince, Gobon Republic of Congo Democratic Republic of Congo, Uganda, Kenya, Somalia, Maldives, Indonesia.
Tropics of Capricorn	South America, Africa, Asia	Chile, Argentina, Paraguay, Brazil, Namibia, Botswana, South Africa, Mozambique, Madagascar, Australia, French Polinesia, Caledonia, Fiji, Tonga and Coolis Island, etc.

Atmosphere

Atmosphere is a mixture of gases.

Gaseous Composition of Atmosphere

Component	Per cent by Volume
Nitrogen	78.08%
Oxygen	20.94%
Argon	0.93%
Carbon dioxide	0.03%
Neon	0.0018%
Helium	0.0005%
Ozone	0.00006%
Hydrogen	0.00005%

Geographical Phenomena

- **Earthquake waves:** Earthquakes generate pulses of energy called **Seismic waves** that can pass through the entire Earth.

Earth's Facts

- **Solstice :** Any of the two occasions, Summer Solstice (21 June) and Winter Solstice (22 December) When the sun is at its highest or lowest point respecitvely in the sky. These occasions are marked by the longest and the shortest days.

- **Equinox :** Any of the two occasions in a year (23 September and 21 March) when days and nights are of equal length throughout the world.

Cyclone

The system of wind rotating inward to an area of low pressure zone from its surrounding high pressure area.

Cyclones	Region
Typhoons	China
Tropical	Indian Ocean
Hurricanes	Caribbean sea
Tornadoes	USA
Willy-Willy	Australia
Taifu	Japan

Tides

- The periodic phenomenon of alternate rise and fall in the sea levels is known as **Tide.**
- It is produced due to gravitational interaction of the Earth, the Moon and the Sun.
- **Spring tides:** On the full moon and the new moon, tides are highest which are called **Spring tides.**

- **Neap tides:** A tide just after the first or third quarters of the moon when there is least difference between high and low water is called **Neap tides.**

Waves

- Waves are the oscillatory movements in water mainly produced by winds, manifested by an alternate rise and fall in the entire sea surface.

Types of Rocks

On the basis of modes of formation there are three types of rocks.

- **Igneous Rocks:** Igneous rock is formed through the cooling and solidification of **magma or lava** such as granite and diorite.
- **Sedimentary Rocks:** Sedimentary rocks are derived from the process of deposition and solidification of sediments after the process of **denudation.** For instance; Sandstone, limestone and chalk rock salts, gypsum or calcium sulphate, etc.
- **Metamorphic Rocks:** Metamorphic rocks arise from the transformation of existing rock types, in a process called **metamorphism**, which means "change in form". Gneiss phyllite, slate, schist, marble, quartzite, etc belongs to the category of metamorphic rocks.

Indian Geography

- **India is the seventh largest** country in the world.
- It covers an area of 32,87,2631 sq. km.
- India is situated North of the Equator between 8°4' and 37°C' North latitude and 68°7' and 97°25' east longitude and is surrounded by the Bay of Bengal in the East, the Arabian sea in the West and the Indian Ocean to the South.

List of Indian State Sharing Border with Neighbour Country

Countries	Indian States
Pakistan	Jammu and Kashmir, Punjab, Rajasthan and Gujrat
China	Jammu and Kashmir, Himachal Pradesh, Uttarakhand, Sikkim and Arunachal Pradesh
Nepal	Bihar, Uttarakhand, Uttar Pradesh, Sikkim and West Bengal
Bangladesh	West Bengal, Mizoram, Meghalaya, Tripura and Asom
Bhutan	West Bengal, Sikkim, Arunachal Pradesh and Asom
Myanmar	Arunachal Pradesh, Nagaland, Manipur and Mizoram
Afghanistan	Jammu and Kashmir (Pakistan occupied area)

Mountain Ranges in India

- The Himalayan Range is the world's highest mountain range.
- The tallest peak of the world, **Mt. Everest**, is also a part of it.
- **Karakoram Range** lies in Jammu and Kashmir and comprises more than 60 peaks.
- K2 (Mount Godwin Austen) is the second highest peak of the world, also a part of this range. Its height is 8611m or 28,251 fit.
- **Shivalik Hills** extend from the Arunachal Pradesh to West Bengal and from Uttarakhand to Kashmir and Himachal Pradesh. Jammu, Kangra and Vaishno Devi are a part of this range.
- **Vindhya Range** spreads across central India and extends across 1,050 km.
- **Aravalli Range** is India's oldest mountain range and spreads across the parts of Rajasthan, Delhi and Haryana. **Guru Shikhar** in **Mount Abu** is the highest peak of this range.
- **Satpura Range** stretches from Gujarat and runs to Maharashtra, Madhya Pradesh and Chhattisgarh.

Mountain Passes of India

Himalayan passes

- **Banihal pass** — between Doda and Anantnag (Jawahar Tunnel), J & K.
- **Shipki La** — River Sutlej enters India from Tibet, Himachal Pradesh.
- **Bara Lachan La** — between Kyelang and Leh, Himachal Pradesh.
- **Rohtang pass** — between Kullu and Kyelang, Himachal Pradesh.
- **Bomdila pass** — between Tezpur and Tawang, Arunachal Pradesh.

Himalayan passes between India and China

- **Shipki La** — Himachal Pradesh.
- **Thaga La and Niti La** — Uttarakhand .
- **Lipu Lekh La** — Tri-junction, India-Nepal-China, Uttarakhand.
- **Jelep La** — Between India and China (Gangtok-Lhasa Road) Sikkim.
- **Nathu La** — Between India and China (Entry to Chumbi Valley) Sikkim.

Trans Himalayan passes
- **Karakoram pass and Aghil pass —** Jammu & Kashmir.

Passes in Western Ghats
- **Palghat** — between Palakkad and Coimbatore.
- **Shenkota** — between Kollam and Madurai.
- **Thalghat** — between Mumbai and Pune.
- **Bhorghat** — between Mumbai and Nasik.

Important Lakes in India

Lakes Name	State
Kolleru Lake, Pulicat Lake	Andhra Pradesh
Deepor Beel, Chandubi Lake, Haflong Lake, Son Beel	Assam
Kanwar Lake	Bihar
Hamirsar Lake, Kankaria Lake, Nal Sarovar, Sursagar Lake	Gujarat
Brighu Lake, Dashir Lake, Dhankar Lake, Kareri (Kumarwah) Lake, Khajjiar Lake, Macchial Lake, Maharana Pratap Sagar, Manimahesh Lake, Nako Lake, Pandoh Lake,	Himachal Pradesh
Prashar Lake, Renuka Lake, Suraj Taal, Chandra Taal	Himacha Pradesh
Badkhal Lake, Brahma Sarovar, Karna Lake, Sannihit Sarovar, Surajkund Lake, Tilyar Lake, Blue Bird Lake	Haryana
Dal Lake, Pangong Tso, Sheshnag Lake	Jammu & Kashmir
Bellandur Lake, Ulsoor Lake, Sankey Lake, Agara Lake, Karanji lake, Kukkarahalli lake, Lingambudhi Lake, Pampa Sarovar	Karnataka
Ashtamudi Lake, Maanaanchira Lake	Kerala
Upper Lake, Lower Lake	Madhya Pradesh
Moti Jheel	Uttar Pradesh
Gorewada Lake, Lonar Lake	Maharashtra
Umiam Lake	Meghalaya
Loktak Lake	Manipur
Palak Dil Lake, Tam Dil Lake	Mizoram
Anshupa Lake, Chilka Lake, Kanjia Lake	Odisha
Kanjli Wetland, Harike Wetland, Ropar Wetland	Punjab

Important Rivers of India

Name	Origin From	Fall into	Length (km)
Ganges	Combined Sources	Bay of Bengal	2525
Satluj	Mansarovar Rakas Lakes	Chenab	1050
Indus	Near Mansarovar Lake	Arabian Sea	2880
Ravi	Kullu Hills near Rohtang Pass	Chenab	720
Beas	Near Rohtang Pass	Satluj	470
Jhelum	Verinag in Kashmir	Chenab	725
Yamuna	Yamunotri	Ganga	1375
Chambal	M.P.	Yamuna	1050
Ghagra	Matsatung Glacier	Ganga	1080
Kosi	Near Gosain Dham Park	Ganga	730
Betwa	Vindhyanchal	Yamuna	480
Son	Amarkantak	Ganga	780
Brahmaputra	Near Mansarovar Lake	Bay of Bengal	2900
Narmada	Amarkantak	Gulf of Khambat	1057
Tapti	Betul Distt. of M.P.	Gulf of Khambat	724
Mahanadi	Raipur Distt. in Chattisgarh	Bay of Bengal	858
Luni	Aravallis	Rann of Kuchchh	450
Ghaggar	Himalayas	Near Fatehabad	494
Sabarmati	Aravallis	Gulf of Khambat	416

Krishna	Western ghats	Bay of Bengal	1327
Godavari	Nasik distt. in Maharashtra	Bay of Bengal	1465
Cauvery	Brahmagir Range of Western Ghats	Bay of Bengal	805
Tungabhadra	Western Ghats	Krishna River	640

Mineral Resources

Aluminium	Kerala.
Antimony	Antimony deposits are found in Punjab and Karnataka.
Asbestos	Karnataka and Rajasthan.
Bauxite	Ranchi and Palamau districts of Jharkhand, Belgaum, Jharia and Thana districts of Maharashtra, Balaghat, Jabalpur, Mandya and Bilaspur districts of Chhattisgarh.
Cement	Katni (M.P.), Lakheri (Rajasthan), Jabalpur (M.P.), Guntur (Andhra Pradesh), Jhinikapani (Singhbhum district of Jharkhand), Surajpur (Haryana).
China Clay	Rajmahal Hills, Singhbhum (district of Jharkhand), Kerala.
Chromite	Singhbhum and Bhagalpur (Jharkhand), Ratnagiri.
Coal	Raniganj (West Bengal), Jharia, Bokaro (Jharkhand), Giridih, Karanpur, Panch Valley and Chanda (M.P.), Singareni (Andhra Pradesh) and Mukum (Assam).
Cobalt	Rajasthan and Kerala.
Copper	Jharkhand (Singhbhum and Barajamda), Chhattisgarh, Rajasthan (**Khetri**).
Diamond	Diamond mines are found in **Panna** district of Madhya Pradesh, **Raipur** district of Chhattisgarh.
Gold	**Kolar** gold-fields (Karnataka).
Graphite	Rajasthan, Andhra Pradesh, Madhya Pradesh, Tamil Nadu, Karnataka, Odisha and Kerala.
Gypsum	Bikaner and Jodhpur (Rajasthan), Tiruchirapalli (Tamil Nadu), Gujarat and Himachal Pradesh.
Iron Ore	Singhbhum (Jharkhand), Chhattisgarh, Keonjhar and Mayurbhanj (Odisha).
Lac	West Bengal.
Lead	Zawar in Udaipur and at the Banjavi mines in Jaipur.
Lignite	Neyveli in South Arcot district (Tamil Nadu).
Limestone	Singareni and Singhbhum (Jharkhand), Panchmahals (Gujarat), Balaghat, Bhandara, Chhindwara, Nagpur.
Manganese	Madhya Pradesh, Jharkhand and Chhattisgarh.
Marble	Jaipur (Rajasthan).
Mica	**Koderma** in Hazaribagh district, Jharkhand, Monghyr.
Petroleum	**Digboi**, Badarpur, Musimpur and Patharia fields of Assam.
Red Stone	Jodhpur (Rajasthan).
Salt	Sambhar Lake (Rajasthan), and ocean water in **Rann of Kutch**.
Silver	Goldfields (Karnataka), Singhbhum.
Tungsten	Bihar, Nagpur (Maharashtra) and Marwar.
Uranium	Bihar.
Zinc	Zawar mines in Udaipur (Rajasthan).

World Geography

- **Asia**

  (43,820,000 sq km) includes 50 countries, and it is the most populated continent, the 60% of the total population of the Earth live here.

- **Africa**

  (30, 370, 000 sq km) comprises 54 countries. It is the hottest continent and home of the world's largest desert, the Sahara, occupying the 25% of the total area of Africa.

- **North America**

  (24, 490,000 sq km) includes 23 countries. Led by the USA as the largest economy in the world.

- **South America**

  (17,840,000 sq km) comprises 12 countries. Here is located the largest forest, the Amazon rainforest, which covers 30% of the South America total area.

- **Antarctica**

  (13,720,000 sq km) is the coldest continent in the world, completely covered with ice. There are no permanent inhabitants, except of scientists maintaining research stations in Antarctica.

- **Europe**

  (10,180,000 sq km) comprises 51 countries. It is the most developed economically continent with the European Union as the biggest economic and political union in the world.

- **Australia**

  (9,008,500 sq km) includes 14 countries. It is the least populated continent after Antarctica, only 0.3% of the total Earth population live here.

List of Ocean in the World

RANK	OCEAN	NOTES
1	Pacific	Separated into north and South pacific.
2.	Atlantic	Separated into north and south Atlantic
3.	Indian	Known as the sea south of India containing the water of Arabian and Laccadive Seas
4.	Southern	Extension of the Pacific, Atlantic and Indian Oceans
5.	Arctic	The sea around North pole containing the water of Greenland sea.

Important Grassland

Regions	Grassland
Australia	Dawns
South America (Argentina & Uruguay)	Pampas
North America	Prairies
Africa and Australia	Savannah
South America	Selvas
Europe and Northern Asia	Steppes
Europe and Asia	Taiga
South Africa	Velds

Longest Rivers

Name, Nation/ Continent	Length in kms	Basin Area m^2 km
Nile Africa	6695	3.25
Amazon, South America	6516	6.14
Yangtze Kiang, China	6380	1.72
Mississippi Missouri, USA	5959	3.20
Ob Irtysh, Russia	5568	2.97
Yenisey Angari a Selenga, Asia	5550	2.55
Yellow (Hwang Ho), China	5464	–
Congo (Zaire), Africa	4667	–
Parana Rio de la Plata, S. Am	4500	2.58

Lakes

Deepest Lakes

Baikal, Russian Fedn	1620 m
Tanganyika, Africa	1463 m
Caspian Sea, Asia-Europe	1025 m
Malawi of Nyasa, Africa	706 m
Issyk-Kul, Kyrgyzstan	702 m

Deserts

Largest Deserts of the World

Subtropical	
Sahara, North Africa	8,600,650 sq. km
Arabian, Middle East	2,300,000 sq. km
Great Victoria, Australia	647,475 sq. km
Kalahari, Southern Africa	582,727 sq. km
Chihuahuan, Mexico	453,232 sq. km
Thar, India/Pakistan	453,232 sq. km
Great Sandy, Australia	388,485 sq. km
Gibson, Australia	310,788 sq. km
Sonoran, S.W. USA	310,788 sq. km
Simpson/Stony, N Africa	145,034 sq. km
Mohave, S.W. USA	139,854 sq. km
Cool Coastal	
Atacama, Chile SA	139,854 sq. km
Namib, S.W. Africa	33,668 sq. km
Cold Winter	
Gobi, China	1,166,450 sq km
Patagonian, Argentina	673,374 sq km
Great Basin, S.W. USA	492,081 sq. km
Kara-kum, West Asia	349,636 sq. km
Colorado, Western USA, also called the Painted Desert	336,687 sq. km
Kyzyl-kum, West Asia	297,838 sq. km
Taklamakan, China	271,939 sq. km
Iranian, Iran	258,990 sq. km

Economy

Economic Planning in India

- **1934:** First attempt to **initiate** economic planning in India was made by **Sir M.Visvesvarayya**, through his book **'Planned Economy For India'**.
- **1938:** 'National Planning Commission' was set up under the chairmanship of **J.L. Nehru** first time.
- **1944:** **'Bombay Plan'** was presented by 8 leading industrialists of Bombay.
- **1944:** **'Gandhian Plan'** was given by S. N. Agarwal.
- **1945:** **'People's Plan'** was given by **M. N. Roy.**
- **1950:** **'Sarvodaya Plan'** was given by **J. P. Narayan.**

The Planning Commission

- It was set up on **March 15, 1950** under the chairmanship J.L. Nehru, by a **resolution** of Union Cabinet.
- It is an extra-constitutional, **non-statutory body.**
- Prime Minister is the ex-officio Chairman, one deputy-Chair appointed by the PM and some full time members.
- In January **2015**, Cabinet **resolution replaced the Planning Commission by NITI Aayog.**

Twelfth Five Year Plan (2012-2017)

Major objective: Faster, Sustainable and More Inclusive Growth.

The main points of the Twelfth Plan are:

Resource Allocation Priorities in 12th plan

- Health and Education received less than projected in Eleventh Plan.
- Infrastructure, including irrigation and watershed management and urban infrastructure, will need additional 0.7 percentage point of GDP over the next 5 years.

National Income

- National Income is the money value of all the final goods & services which produced by a country during one year.
- India is now the world's 3rd largest economy in terms of real prices and purchasing power.

Measures/Concepts of National Income

1. Gross Domestic Product (GDP)

GDP is the total money value of all final goods & services produced within the geographical boundaries of the country (produced by resident citizens + foreign nationals) during a given period of time, generally one year.

$$GDP = Q \times P,$$

Q = Total quantity of final goods & services.
P = Price of final goods & services.

2. Gross National Product (GNP)

GNP is the money value of total output or production of final goods & services produced by the nationals of a country during a given period of time, generally a year. In this case, the income of all the resident & non-resident citizens of a country is included whereas the income of foreign nationals who reside within the geographical boundary of the country is excluded.

$$GNP = GDP + (X - M)$$

X = Export of goods & services
M = Import of goods & services
X – M = Net Factor Income from Abroad (NFIA)

So, $$GNP = GDP + NFIA$$

3. Net National Product (NNP): can be calculated in 2 ways:-

(i) NNP at market price:

$$NNP = GNP - Depreciation$$

Depreciation means wear & tear of goods produced.
NNP at market price includes Indirect taxes and excludes subsidies.

(ii) NNP at factor cost: NNP at factor cost calculates National Income only on the basis of cost incurred to produce the goods & services. This cost is the payment made to the factors of production.

$$NNP_{fc} = NNP_{mp} - Indirect\ Taxes + Subsidy$$

When NNP is obtained at factor cost, it is known as National Income.

Likewise, GDP at factor cost also can be calculated.

$$GDP_{fc} = GDP_{mp} - \text{Indirect Taxes} + \text{Subsidy}$$

4. Personal Income

It is that income which is actually obtained by nationals in one year.

P.I. = National Income – Undistributed Profits of Corporation – Payments for Social Security Provisions – Corporate Taxes + Government Transfer payments + Business Transfer payments + Net Interest paid by government.

SOCIAL SECURITY PROVISIONS = Payments made by employees towards pension & provident fund

TRANSFER PAYMENTS = Payments made not against any productive activity. eg. – old age pension, unemployment compensation, disaster relief payment, etc.

5. Disposal Personal Income (DPI)

Income that is available to individuals that can be disposed at their will.

$$DPI = \text{Personal Income} - \text{Direct Taxes.}$$

6. National Income at constant price & current price

NI CONSTANT PRICE = Total quantity of all final goods & services produced in a particular year × Price of base year.

Base year of National Income accounts is the year chosen to enable inter – year comparisons. The new series changes the base to 2011–12 from 2004–05

NI CURRENT PRICE = Total quantity of all final goods & services produced in a particular year × Price of goods & services in that particular year.

Budget

Budget is an annual financial statement. The Budget in India is divided into 2 parts – Revenue Account & Capital Account.

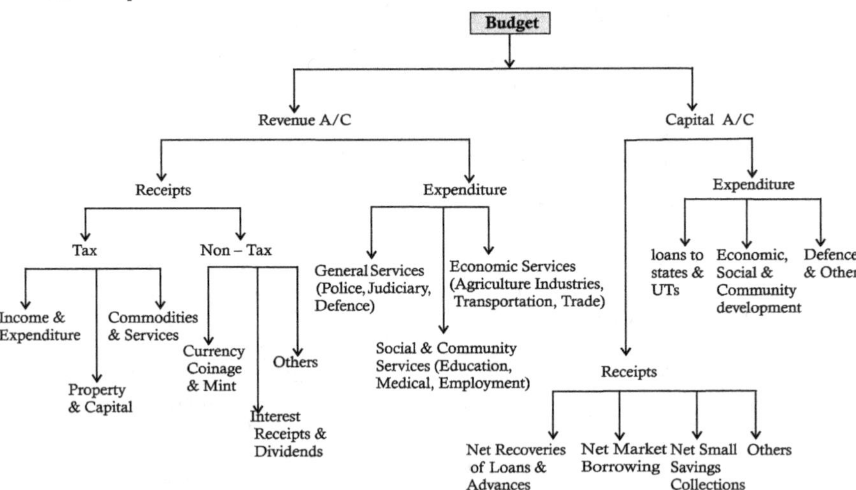

Indian Tax Structure

- **Tax Structure** present in India is very strong and follows the financial year.
- **Direct taxes** are those which are imposed on a person either on his income or wealth and the tax liability cannot be escaped. It is governed by Central Board of Direct Taxes (CBDT).
- **Indirect tax** is collected by middle men in the channels of distribution of goods and it is remitted to the Government treasury. It is governed by Central Board of Excise and Customs (CBEC).

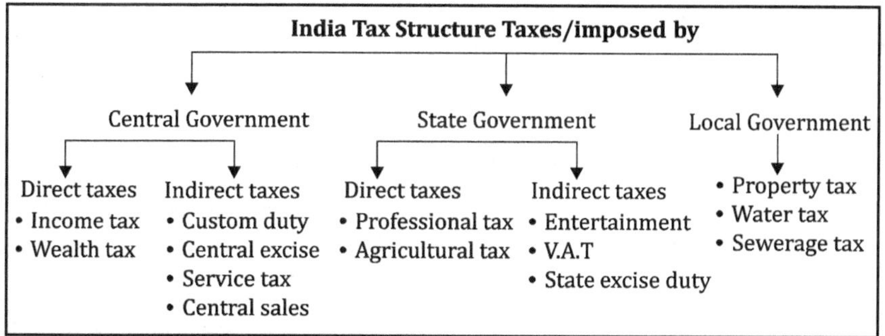

Goods and Services Tax (GST)

Features

- Uniform regim of taxes across India.
- Common market of goods and services across India.
- States will collect services taxes.
- Centre will collect Integrated Goods and Service Tax (IGST) or inter-state supplies.
- IGST rate will be equal to Central GST (CGST) + State GST (SGST).
- It will subsume 16 central or state's taxes.
- **GST structure :** 5%, 12%, 18% & 28%

  Cess Surcharge : Luxury cars-15%; Aerated drink & water–15%; Pan masala – 135%; Tobacco & Cigarettes–290%.

GST Replaces

States Taxes		Central Taxes	
•	VAT/Sales Tax	•	Central Excise Duty
•	Entry Tax/Octroi	•	Excise Duty on Medicines and Toilet
•	Local Tax	•	Additional Custom Duty
•	Entertainment Tax	•	Sp. Add. Custom Duty
•	Purchase Tax	•	Countervailing Duty
•	Mandi Tax/Local Levls	•	Service Tax
•	Luxury Tax	•	Cesses and surcharges
•	Tax on Lottery and Betting		
•	Inter-state Tax		

Poverty

Poverty

Poverty can be defined as a social phenomenon in which a section of the society is unable to fulfil even its basic necessities of life.

Magnitude of Poverty in India

The Planning Commission of India has estimated rural and urban poverty in India from the sixth Five Year Plan ownwards.

Type of Poverty

1. Absolute
2. Relative

Unemployment in India

Unemployment

In broad sense a state of unemployment appears when a labour does not obtain employment opportunity despite his willingness to work on existing wage rate.

Different Types of Unemployment in India

1. Structural Unemployment

This type of unemployment is associated with economic structure of the country, i.e. rapidly growing population, technological change and their immobility fall in rate of capital formation.

2. Under-employment

The labourers are under-employed who obtain work but their efficiency and capability are not utilised at their optimum and as a result they contribute in the production upto a limited level.

Schemes for Women and Child Development

1. Ahimsa Messengers
- Scheme of Ministry of women and child development launched by UPA in 2013.
- Includes Women Panchayati Raj Members, Youth, NGOs etc.
- These people work for prevention of violence against women, dowry etc.

2. CSWB
- Central social welfare board (CSWB).
- To implement welfare programs for women and children via NGOs, family counselling, awareness generation etc.

3. Poorna Shakti Kendra
- Created under National Mission for empowerment of women in 2013.
- One stop information centres.
- Help women get benefit from various govt. schemes.

4. SABLA
- Rajiv Gandhi Scheme for Empowerment of Adolescent Girls launched in 2011.
- To provide nutrition for growing adolescent girls by provision of food grains.
- All girls will be given a kishori card which will be updated with details of the girl's growth and provision of the food grains.
- SABLA is created by merging earlier two schemes: Nutrition program for adolescent girls + Kishori Shakti Yojana.
- Target: girls aged 11-18.
- 100 gms of foodgrain per day per girl for 300 days in a year.

5. Saksham
- This is a scheme by Ministry of Women and Child Development launched in 2012.
- Made due to rising demand for gender sensitisation among boys after the Delhi gang-rape incident.
- It'll give training/moral education to adolescent boys (11-18 age) to respect women.

6. STEP
- Support to Training and Employment program for Women.
- Provides skill training.

Child labour v/s Right to Education (RTE)
- RTE = Every child between the ages of 6 and 14 has right to free (and compulsory) elementary education
- Child Labour (Prohibition and Regulation) Act of 1986 makes a distinction between hazardous and non-hazardous categories of work for children under 14 years.

National Rural Health Mission
- Focus will be post-menopausal problems, osteoporosis and breast and cervical cancer.
- Dovetailing of NRHM with IGMSY [Indra Gandhi Matritva Sahyog Yojana] (conditional cash transfer for maternity benefit) and National Food Security Bill (NFSB) will be undertaken.
- Training Anganwadi and ASHA workers (Accredeted Social Health Activist) on issues relating to nutrition, counselling, child rights and gender discrimination

Rashtriya Bal Swasthya Karyakram
- This scheme was launched in 2013.
- To provide comprehensive healthcare and improve the quality of life of children focus on 4D.
- Defects at birth (cleft lip, down's syndrome, Talipes etc.).
- Diseases (dental, heart, asthama etc.).

ICDS
- Integrated Child Development Service (ICDS) started in 1975.
- Beneficiary-children below the age of six, lactating mothers, pregnant mothers.

Dhanlakshmi
Conditional cash transfer for girl child, launched in 2008, for fulfilling following conditions:
- birth and registration of birth
- immunization
- enrolment and retention in school

Rajiv Gandhi National Creche
- Scheme provides for day-care facilities to 0-6 year-old children of working mothers by opening crèches and development services
- Requirement: combined monthly income of both the parents should not exceed ₹12,000 for availing of the facilities.

Industries
- Public Sector Enterprises (PSE) is a government-owned corporation owned by Union Government of India, or one of the many state or territorial governments, or both.
- They are under the Department of Public Enterprises of Ministry of Heavy Industries and Public Enterprises.
- There are 298 PSU companies on 31-03-2015 in India.

- **Maharatna**
- **Navratna**
- **Miniratna**

CPSEs (itself divided into Category I & Category II)

Currently here are 8 Maharatna, 16 Navratna and 75 Miniratna CPSE's.

There are 8 Maharatnas :

(i)   Bharat Heavy Electricals (BHEL)
(ii)   Coal India Limited
(iii) Indian Oil Corporation (IOC)
(iv)   GAIL (India) Limited
(v)   NTPC Limited
(vi)   Oil & Natural Gas Corporation (ONGC) Ltd.
(vii) Steel Authority of India (SAIL) Ltd.

There are **16 Navratna** CPSEs in the country, these are:

1.   Bharat Electronics Limited
2.   Container Corporation of India Limited
3.   Engineers India Limited
4.   Hindustan Aeronautics Limited
5.   Hindustan Petroleum Corporation Limited
6.   Mahanagar Telephone Nigam Limited
7.   National Aluminium Company Limited
8.   National Buildings Construction Corporation Limited
9.   NMDC Limited
10. Neyveli Lignite Corporation Limited
11. Oil India Limited
12. Power Finance Corporation Limited
13. Power Grid Corporation of India Limited
14. Rashtriya Ispat Nigam Limited
15. Rural Electrification Corporation Limited
16. Shipping Corporation of India Limited

Classification of Industries:

A. On the basis of source of raw materials

- **Agro based industry** (cotton textile, jute textile and sugar).
- **Mineral based industry** (iron and steel, machine tools and aluminium).

B. On the basis of main role played by the industry

- **Basic industries:** these are the industries whose finished products are used as the raw materials for other industries.
- **Consumer goods industries:** these are the industries whose finished products are directly used for consumption by consumers.

C. On the basis of capital investment

- **Small scale** industry
- **Large scale** industry

D. On the basis of ownership

- **Public sector undertaking**
  (SAIL, HAL, BEML)
- **Private sector undertaking**
  (TISCO, Mahindra and Mahindra, Birla Cement)
- **Joint sector undertaking**
  (Oil India Limited)
- **Co-operative industries**
  (Sugar Industry in Maharashtra)

E. Based on the bulk of raw materials and finished products

- Heavy industries
- Light industries

In India, industries are concentrated in four main regions:

1. West Bengal, Jharkhand and Chhatisgarh
2. Maharashtra and Gujarat region
3. Gangetic Plains
4. South India

Banking in India

The State Bank of India is the largest commercial bank in India.

Reserve Bank of India

- **Central bank** of India.
- **Established on April 1, 1935** with a capital of ₹ 5 crore.
- **Nationalised on January 1, 1949** as Government acquired the private share holdings.
- **Administration:** 14 Directors in Central Board of Directors besides the Governor, 4 Deputy Governors and 1 Government official. The Governor is the Chairman of the Board and Chief Executive of the Bank.

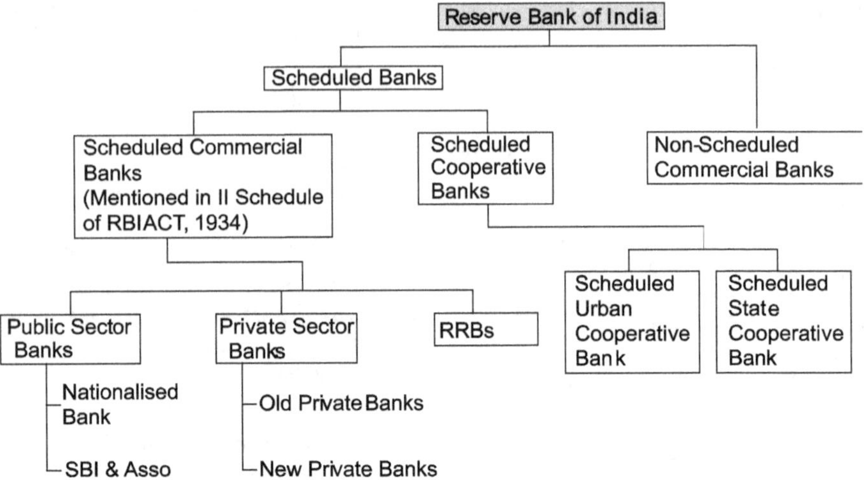

- **Governors:** 1st Governor of RBI – Sir Smith (1935-37); 1st Indian Governor- CD Deshmukh (1948-49).
- RBI follows Minimum Reserve System worth 200 crore (₹ 115 crore gold & ₹ 85 crore bond).
- All notes except one rupee are issued by the RBI & bear the signature of RBI Governor.
- Where as the one rupee note bears signature of Secretary of Finance (GOI).
- No personal accounts are maintained & operated in RBI.

Functions of RBI

- Issuance of note.
- Banker to the Government.
- Banker's Bank.
- Controller of Credit
- Custodian of Foreign Reserves
- Formulates and administers the monetary policy in India.
- Acts as the agent of the Government of India in respect to India's membership of the IMF and the World Bank.
- RBI acts as the central clearing house for the inter bank transactions.
- **Credit control** means control over the quantity and value of credit in the country. Among the functions of Central Bank, one main function is to control and regulate the credit in the country.

1. **Quantitative Credit Control:**
   Bank Rate, Cash Reserve Ratio (CRR), Open Market Operations (OMO), Statutory Liquidity Ratio (SLR), Repo/Reserve Repo.

2. **Qualitative Credit Control:**
   Rationing of Credit, Regulation of Credit for Consumption Purpose, Variation of margin requirements, Moral Control, Direct action.

Printing Press in India

India Security Press (Nashik Road): Postal Material, Postal Stamps, Non-postal Stamps, Judicial and Non-judicial Stamps, Cheques, Bonds, NSC, Kisan Vikas Patra, Securities of State Governments, Public Sector Enterprise and Financial Corporations.

Currency Notes Press (Nashik Road): Since 1991, this press prints currency notes of ₹ 1, ₹ 2, ₹ 5, ₹ 10, ₹ 50, and ₹ 100.

Bank Notes Press (Dewas): Currency notes of ₹20, ₹50, ₹100 and ₹500 are printed here.

Modernized Currency Notes Press: Two new modernized currency notes press are under establishment at Mysore (Karnataka) and Salboni (West Bengal).

Security Paper: Hoshangabad (established in 1967-68) makes production of Bank and Currency notes paper.

Coins are minted at four places: Mumbai, Kolkata, Hyderabad and Noida.

Stock Exchange of India

- The Securities Contracts (Regulation) Act of 1956 established for the purpose of assisting, regulating and controlling, business in buying, selling and dealing in securities."

- There are **24 stock exchanges** in India.

> Bombay Stock Exchange 1875- one of the oldest in the world and oldest in Asia.
>
> Madras Stock Exchange- 1920
>
> Ahmedabad Stock Exchange- 1894
>
> Calcutta Stock Exchange- 1908
>
> Securities and Exchange Board of India (SEBI): April 1988

SEBI

- It was given statutory status and powers through an ordinance promulgated on January 30, 1992.
- **Its office is situated in Mumbai** with regional offices at Delhi, Chennai and Calcutta.

Functions of SEBI:
- Check insider trading of securities.
- Encourage self-regulatory organisations.
- Eliminate malpractice of security market.
- Safeguard interests of investors.

Agriculture

The agriculture sector of India occupies almost 43% of India's geographical area.

Importance

- It is the 19% contributor to India's GDP.
- Provides livelihood to 65-70% of total population and employment to 58.4% of total work force.
- Importance source of raw materials to large and small scale industries.
- Agriculture accounts for 14.7% of total export earnings.
- Agriculture and related products contribute to 38% in total exports of the country.

Food grains procurement and Stocks in India

Food grains procurement by government serves two purposes- providing support price to the farmers and building up public stocks of food grains. It is carried by Food Corporation of India **(FCI)**.

- Market intervention to augment supply so as to help moderate the open market prices.

Green Revolution in India

- The term 'green revolution' was given by American scientist- Dr. William Gande.
- The credit of Green Revolution goes to **Dr. Norman Borlaug (Mexico)** and **Dr. M.S. Swaminathan in India.**

Second Green Revolution in India

- Strategy adopted in Eleventh Plan.

- It aimed at efficient use of resources and conservation of soil, water and ecology on a sustainable basis and in a holistic framework.

Other Revolutions	
Revolution	**Area**
Yellow Revolution	Oil Seeds
White Revolution	Milk
Blue Revolution	Fish
Pink Revolution	Shrimp
Grey Revolution	Fertiliser
Golden Revolution	Horticulture

White Revolution and Operation Flood in India

- India stands first in the world in the milk production.
- **Dr. Varghese Kurien is the pioneer of operation flood in India.**

Foreign Direct Investment (FDI)

Foreign Direct Investment (FDI) is an investment in a business by an investor from another country for which the foreign investor has control over the company purchased.

- A Multi National Enterprise (MNE) may create a new foreign enterprise by making a direct investment, which is called a *greenfield investment.*
- A MNE may make a direct investment by the acquisition of a foreign firm, which is called an *acquisition* or *prownfield investment.*
- The Government has allowed 100% FDI in all the sectors except Space (74%), Defence (49%), and News Media (26%).
- FDI restrictions in tea plantation has been removed.

Financial Inclusion

The objective of Financial Inclusion is to extend financial services to the large hitherto un-served population of the country to unlock its growth potential. Following are the

1. Expansion of Bank Branch Network.
2. Swabhimaan Scheme
3. Direct Benefit Transfer
4. PAHAL Scheme
5. Pradhan Mantri Jan-Dhan Yojana (PMJDY)
   PMJDY was formally launched on 28th August, 2014.

New Pension System

The National Pension System (NPS) was launched on 1ˢᵗ January, 2004 with the objective of providing retirement income to all the citizens. It is a co-contributory pension scheme, **'Swavalamban Scheme'** in the Union Budget of 2010-11, under which the Government will contribute a sum of ₹ 1,000 to each eligible NPS subscriber who contributes a minimum of ₹ 1,000 & maximum ₹ 12,000 per annum.

Glossary

- **Ante date:** To give a date prior to that on which it is written, to any cheque, bill or any other document.
- **Ad valorem tax-** a tax based on the value of property.
- **Balance of trade (or payment):** The difference between the visible exports and visible imports of two countries in trade with each other is called balance of payment.
- **Basis Point:** A unit of measurement which is equal to 1/100th of 1%. This is used to measure changes in interest rates, stock-market indices or yield on fixed income securities.
- **Balance Sheet:** It is a statement of accounts, generally of a business concern, prepared at the end of a year.
- **Bank Rate:** It is the rate of interest charged by the Reserve Bank of India for lending money to Commercial Banks.
- **Bear:** A speculator in the stock market who believes that prices will go down.
- **Bull:** Speculators in the stock markets who buy goods, in some cases without money to pay with, anticipating that prices will go up.
- **Cartel:** It is a combination of business, generally in the same trade formed with a view to controlling prices and enjoy monopoly.
- **Call money:** Loan made for a very short period. It carries a very low rate of interest.
- **Commercial Banks:** Financial institutions that create credit, accept deposits, give loans and perform other financial functions.

- **Deferred Payment:** Payments put off to a future date or extended over a period of time. Interest will usually still accumulates during deferment.
- **Deflation:** Deflation is a reduction in the level of national income and output, usually accompanied by a fall in the general price level.
- **Depreciation:** Reduction in the value of fixed assets due to wear and tear.
- **Devaluation:** Official reduction in the foreign value of domestic currency. It is done to encourage the country's exports and discourage imports.
- **Dividend:** Earning of stock paid to shareholders.
- **Dumping:** Sale of a commodity at different prices in different markets, lower price being charged in the market where demand is relatively elastic.
- **Double Taxation:** Corporate earnings taxed at both the corporate level and again as a stock holder dividend.
- **Fiscal policy:** Government's expenditure and tax policy.
- **Free-trade Area:** A form of economic integration in which there exists free internal trade among member countries but each member is free to levy different external tariffs against non-member nations.
- **Payee (Drawee):** The person who receives a payment. This often applies to cheque.
- **Payer (Drawer):** The person who makes a payment. This often applies to cheque.
- **Repo Rate:** The rate at which banks borrow from RBI. It injects liquidity into the market.
- **Reverse Repo Rate:** The rate at which RBI borrows from banks for a short-term. It withdraws liquidity from the market.
- **Statutory Liquidity Ratio (SLR):** SLR is the portion that banks need to invest in the form of cash, gold or government approved securities.
- **VAT(Value Added Tax):** A form of indirect sales tax paid on products and services at each stage of production or distribution, based on the value added at that stage and included in the cost to the ultimate customer.

Banking in India

Banking is defined as accepting for the purpose of lending or investment of depositors money. The banks are the custodians of savings and powerful institutions to provide credit and mobilise the resources from all the sections of the community byway of deposits and channelise them to industries/related sectors.

The first bank in India was 'Bank of Hindustan' started in 1770 by Alexander & Co., an English agency house in Calcutta, which failed in 1782 with the closure of the agency house. The East India Company established 3 Banks-Bank of Bengal (1809), Bank of Bombay (1840) and Bank of Madras (1843). These Banks continued their smooth operations till 1920 when they were amalgamated to form Imperial Bank of India, which was formally established on January 27, 1921.

Thirty four years later after the passing of the State Bank of India Act, 1955, this Imperial Bank was taken over by the State Bank of India.

The Government of India on the recommendations of the banking commission nationalised 14 major commercial banks on July 19, 1969 (Phase-I), and 6 additional banks on April 15, 1980 (Phase-II).

Nationalisation Phase -I

- Central Bank of India Ltd
- Bank of India Ltd
- Punjab National Bank Ltd
- The Bank of Baroda Ltd.
- The Corporation Bank Ltd.
- Canara Bank Ltd.
- United Bank of India Ltd.

- Dena Bank Ltd
- Syndicate Bank Ltd
- The Union Bank of India Ltd
- Allahabad Bank Ltd.
- The Indian Bank Ltd.
- The Bank of Maharashtra Ltd.
- The Indian Overseas Bank Ltd.

Nationalisation Phase-II

- The Andhra Bank Ltd.
- The Punjab & Sind Bank Ltd.
- The New Bank of India Ltd.
- The Vijaya Bank Ltd.
- The United Commercial Bank Ltd.
- The Oriental Bank of Commerce Ltd.

Regional Rural Banks (RRBs)

RRBs were established in 1975 following recommendations of Narsimham Committee Working Report.

The main purpose was to include rural areas into economic mainstream since majority of India resides in rural areas. The RRBs were owned by Central Government (50%), Sponsor bank (35%) and respective State governments (15%). RRB's are going through a process of amalgamation and consolidation and in the near future more RRB will merge with other RRB in the state. The area of operation of RRBs is limited to the area as notified by Government of India covering one or more state districts.

RRBs perform various functions including Providing banking facilities to rural and semi-urban areas, carrying out government operations like disbursement of wages of beneficiaries of government schemes etc.

Prathma bank was first RRB of India established on 2nd October 1975.

Agriculture in India

- Agriculture, with its allied sectors (e.g. animal husbandry, fisheries, horticulture, dairying, sericulture, pisciculture etc.) is the largest livelihood provider in India.
- It contributes a significant figure to the GDP. Agriculture, forestry & fishing sector is estimated to grow by 3.8 percent (GVA at Basic Prices for 2018-19) as compared to growth of 3.4 percent in 2017-18.
- Indian agriculture and allied activities have witnessed a green revolution, a white revolution, a yellow revolution and a blue revolution.
- India has three major cropping seasons – Rabi, Kharif and Zaid
- Rabi (sown in winter - October to December and harvested in summer – March to April.) e.g. wheat, barley, peas, gram, mustard.
- Kharif (sown during monsoon-July/August and harvested in September-October) e.g. paddy, maize, jowar, bajra, arhar, moong, urad, cotton, jute, groundnut, soyabean
- Zaid (Short summer period –April to June between Rabi and Kharif seasons) e.g. watermelon, muskmelon, cucumber

Crops	Major producing states
Wheat	Uttar Pradesh, Punjab and Madhya Pradesh
Rice	West Bengal, Uttar Pradesh, Andhra Pradesh
Maize	Andhra Pradesh, Karnataka, Rajasthan
Millets	Rajasthan, Maharashtra, Gujarat
Barley	Maharashtra, Uttar Pradesh, Rajasthan
Jute	West Bengal, Bihar
Cotton	Gujarat, Maharashtra
Coconut	Kerala, Tamil Nadu
Rapeseed	Rajasthan, Madhya Pradesh
Coffee	Karnataka, Kerala
Tea	Assam, West Bengal, Kerala, Tamil Nadu
Rubber	Kerala, Tamil Nadu
Tobacco	Andhra Pradesh, Telangana, Karnataka
Pepper	Kerala, Karnataka, Tamil Nadu
Turmeric	Telangana, Tamil Nadu, Odisha

Agro-climatic zones of India

Agro-climatic Zones	States
Western Himalayan region	Himachal Pradesh, Jammu & Kashmir, Uttarakhand
Eastern Himalayan region	Arunachal Pradesh, Assam, Manipur, Meghalaya, Mizoram, Nagaland, Sikkim, Tripura, West Bengal
Lower Gangetic plain region	West Bengal
Middle Gangetic plain region	Uttar Pradesh, Bihar
Upper Gangetic plain region	Uttar Pradesh
Trans Gangetic plain region	Chandigarh, Delhi, Haryana, Punjab, Rajasthan
Eastern plateau and hills region	Chhattisgarh, Jharkhand, Madhya Pradesh, Maharashtra, Odisha, West Bengal
Central plateau and hills region	Madhya Pradesh, Rajasthan, Uttar Pradesh
Western plateau and hills region	Madhya Pradesh, Maharashtra
Southern plateau and hills region	Andhra Pradesh, Karnataka, Tamil Nadu
East coast plains and hills region	Andhra Pradesh, Odisha, Puducherry, Tamil Nadu
West coast plains and ghat region	Goa, Karnataka, Kerala, Maharashtra, Tamil Nadu
Gujarat plains and hills region	Gujarat, Dadra & Nagar Haveli, Daman & Diu
Western dry region	Rajasthan
Island region	Andaman & Nicobar Islands, Lakshadweep

Schemes & Policies

Important Schemes by Government of India

Pradhan Mantri Kisan Samman Nidhi (PM-KISAN)

To extend direct income support at the rate of ₹6,000 per year to farmer families, having cultivable land up to 2 hectares.

Under this Scheme, ₹2,000 each will be transferred to the bank accounts of around 12 crore Small and Marginal farmer families, in three equal instalments.

This programme would be made effective from 1st December 2018 and the first instalment for the period up to 31st March 2019 would be paid during 2019.

Pradhan Mantri Shram-Yogi Maandhan (PM-SYM)

To provide pensions to the workers of unorganized sector of the country.

In this scheme in addition to workers of un-organized sectors, workers of similar other occupations whose monthly income is ₹15,000/ per month or less and belong to the entry age group of 18-40 years are eligible

Each subscriber under the PM-SYM, shall receive minimum assured pension of ₹3000/- per month after attaining the age of 60 years

During the receipt of pension, if the subscriber dies, the spouse of the beneficiary shall be entitled to receive 50% of the pension received by the beneficiary as family pension.

Ayushman Bharat -Pradhan Mantri Jan Aarogya Yojana (AB-PMJAY)

Cover of up to ₹5 lakhs per family per year, for secondary and tertiary care hospitalization.

Cashless and paperless access to services for the beneficiary at the point of service.

World's largest government funded healthcare program targeting more than 50 crore beneficiaries (10.74 crore vulnerable families) - When fully implemented

Pradhan Mantri UjjwalaYojana (PMUY)

To provide clean cooking fuel to BPL households in the country. Under this scheme 5 Crore deposit-free LPG connections were targeted to women belonging to BPL families.

Subsequently target was increased to 8 Crore with a budgetary allocation of ₹12800 crore.

Initial target of 5 crore connections achieved well before the target i.e.31st March, 2019. Crossed 6 crore mark in January 2019. Beneficiaries are identified from categories i.e. SC/STs households, beneficiaries of Pradhan Mantri Awas Yojana (PMAY (Gramin), Antodaya Anna Yojana (AAY), Forest dwellers, Most backward Classes (MBC), Tea & Ex-Tea Garden Tribes and people residing in Islands/ river islands.

Deen Dayal Upadhyaya Grameen Kaushalya Yojana (DDU-GKY)

To cater the career aspirations of rural youth and adding diversity to the incomes of rural poor families and transform rural poor youth into an economically independent and globally relevant workforce

Mainly focused on rural youth between the ages of 15 and 35 years from poor families to be a part of skilled workforce of the country

As a part of the Skill India campaign, it plays an instrumental role in supporting the social and economic programs of the government like the Make in India, Digital India, Smart Cities and Start-Up India, Stand-Up India campaigns.

Startup India

To build a strong ecosystem that is conducive for the growth of startup businesses, to drive sustainable economic growth and generate large scale employment opportunities.

The Government through this initiative aims to empower startups to grow through innovation and design.

The 19-Point Startup India Action Plan envisages several incubation centres, easier patent filing, tax exemptions, ease of setting-up of business, a INR 10,000 Crore corpus fund, and a faster exit mechanism

Stand Up India Scheme

To promote entrepreneurship amongst women, SC & ST category. The scheme facilitates in providing bank loans between Rs.10 lakh and Rs.1 crore to at least one Scheduled Caste/ Scheduled Tribe borrower and at least one Woman borrower per bank branch for setting up greenfield enterprises. Apart from providing credit facility, Stand Up India Scheme also envisages extending hand-holding support to the potential borrowers.

General Science

Physics is the branch of science which deals with the study of matter, energy, and the interaction between them.
- A **scalar** is a physical quantity that has only a magnitude (size) E.g. : Distance, speed, time, power, energy, etc.
- A **vector** is a physical quantity that has both a magnitude and a direction. E.g. Velocity, displacement, acceleration, force etc.

Some physical quantities like moment of **inertia**, **stress**, etc. are neither scalar nor vector. They are **tensor**.

Seven Fundamental Physical Quantities and their Units

Physical Quantity	SI Unit	Symbol
Length	meter	m
Mass	kilogram	Kg
Time	second	S
Electric Current	ampere	A
Temperature	kelvin	K
Luminous intensity	candela	Cd
Amount of substance	mole	mol

Some Derived Physical Quantities and their Units

S. No	Physical Quantity	cgs unit	SI unit	Relation
1.	Force	dyne	newton	1 newton = 10^5 dyne
2.	Work	erg	joule	1 joule = 10^7 erg

Motion

- **First law of Motion** - An object at rest will remain at rest or in uniform motion remains in uniform motion unless acted on by an external unbalanced force.

  This law is often called the law of inertia. i.e., resistance to change.
- **Second law of Motion** - The rate of change of momentum of a body is directly proportional to the unbalanced external force applied on it.
- **Third law of Motion** - For every action there is an equal and opposite reaction.

Circular Motion

- Motion of a body along a circular path is called circular motion.
- **Centripetal force** - while a body is moving along a circular path an external force required to act radially inward.

  A pseudo force that is equal and opposite to the centripetal force is called **centrifugal force.**

Cream separator, centrifugal dryer, etc, work on the principle of centrifugal force.

Friction

Friction is a force that is created whenever two surfaces move or try to move across each other. Friction always opposes the motion or attempted motion of one surface across another surface.

Instances where friction is important
Walking , Driving ,Picking something up, Car brakes,

Work, Energy & Powers

Work

- **Work** refers to an activity involving a force and movement in the direction of the force.

Energy

Capacity of doing work is called *energy*.
- It may exist in potential, kinetic, thermal, electrical, chemical, nuclear, or other various forms.

- Energy cannot be created or destroyed. It can only be transferred to other objects or converted into different forms. This is **Law of Conservation of energy.**
- The SI unit of energy is joule.
- The energy associated with motion is called **kinetic energy (K).**
- The energy associated with position is called **potential energy (U).**

Conversion of Energy

Dynamo-	Mechanical Energy into Electrical Energy.
Electric Motor-	Electrical Energy into - Mechanical Energy.
Microphone-	Sound Energy into Electrical Energy.
Loud Speaker-	Electrical Energy into Sound Energy.
Electric Bulb-	Electrical Energy into Light and Heat Energy.
Solar Cell–	Solar energy into electrical energy.

Power

- **Power** is the rate of doing work.
- Power = Work / time
- The **SI** unit of **power** is **joule/second.**
- **One horse** power = **746** watt.

Gravitation

- **Gravitation** is a natural phenomenon by which all physical bodies attract each other.
- On Earth, gravity gives weight to physical objects employing a downward force to keep them grounded.
- According to Newton's theory, the gravitational attraction between the planets and the sun holds the planets in elliptical orbits around the sun.
- The force of gravity depends upon the **object's mass** or the amount of matter in the object.
- The weight (w) of an object is equal to the mass of the object multiplied by the acceleration due to gravity(g).
  $W = mg$
- $g_{maximum}$ at poles and $g_{minimum}$ at equator.
- $g_{moon} = 1/6\ g_{earth}$
- The value of 'g' decreases with altitude, depth from the earth's surface.
- **g** decreases due to rotation of earth.
- **Escape speed (v_e)** is the minimum speed with which an object just crosses the earth's gravitational field and never comes back.
- The escape velocity of Earth is about 11.2 kilometres per second and on moon it is 2.4 km/sec.

Satellites

- A **satellite** is a smaller object in space which orbits around a larger object Planet in space.
- It can be either artificial, like the communication or weather satellites that orbit the Earth, or they can be natural, like our Moon.
- A **geostationary satellite** is an earth-orbiting satellite, placed at an altitude of approximately 35,800 kilometres (22,300 miles) directly over the equator.

Solids and Fluids

- **Elasticity and plasticity:** The property by virtue of which the body regains its original shape after the removal of deforming force is called **elasticity.** And if the body retains its deformed shape after the removal of deforming force is called **plasticity.**
- **Rubber** is less elastic than steel.
- **Pressure** is defined as force acting normally on an unit area of the surface.
  Its unit is N/m^2. It is a scalar quantity.
- **Atmospheric pressure** is measured by
- **Sudden fall** in barometric reading in the indication of **storm.**
- **Slow fall** in barometric reading is the indication of **rain.**
- **Slow rise** in the barometric reading is the indication of clear weather.

Atmospheric Pressure Decreases with Altitude

- It is difficult to cook on the mountain.
- The **fountain pen** of a passenger leaks in aeroplane.
- **Bleeding** occurs from the nose of the man.
- It is difficult to breath on higher altitude due to less amount of air.
- **Water** starts to boil below **100°C.**

Archimedes' Principle

When a body is immersed partly or wholly in a liquid, there is an apparent loss in the weight of the body, which is equal to the weight of liquid displaced by the body.

- All objects placed in a liquid experience an upward force called the **buoyant force** and the law is called the **law of buoyancy.**
- The weight of water displaced by an iron ball is less than its own weight. Whereas water displaced by the immersed portion of a ship is equal to its weight. So, small ball of iron ball sink in water, but large ship float.
- **Density of water** is maximum at **4°C.**

Heat

- **Heat** is a form of energy which causes sensation of hotness or coldness.
  Its unit is joule or calorie.
- 1 cal = 4.2 joule
- It always flows from a substance at a higher temperature to the substance at a lower temperature.

Temperature

It indicates the degree of hotness or coldness of a body.
- Temperature is measured by **thermometer**.

Relation between Temperature on different scales.

$$\frac{C}{5} = \frac{F-32}{9} = \frac{R}{4} = \frac{K-273}{5} = \frac{Ra-492}{9}$$

- The normal temperature of a human body is 37°C or 98.6°F.
- At –40° temperature, celsius and fahrenheit thermometers read the same.

Conduction

It is that mode of transmission of heat in solid where heat is transferred from a region of higher temperature to a region of lower temperature by the aid of particles of the body without their actual migration.

Convection

It requires a medium and is the process in which heat is transferred from one place to other by actual movement of heated substance (usually molecule of fluid).

Radiation

Has the following properties:
(a) Radiant energy travels in straight lines and when some object is placed in the path, its shadow is formed at the detector.
(b) It is reflected and refracted or can be made to interfere.
(c) It can travel through vacuum.

Latent Heat

- The amount of heat required to change phase (liquid to gas or liquid to solid etc.) without change in temperature is called **latent heat.**

Specific Heat

- The amount of heat that is required to raise the temperature of a unit mass of a substance by one degree (14.5°C to 15.5°C) is known as **Specific heat.**

Sublimation

It is the process of conversion of a solid directly into vapour, eg., Iodine (dark solid), Dry ice (solid CO_2), etc.

Hoar Frost: It is just the reverse process of sublimation. e.g. Frost and snowflakes.

Waves

- A **wave** is a kind of oscillation (disturbance) that travels through space and matter.
- Wave motions transfer energy, not matter from one place to another.
- **Transverse wave**- In it the vibrations of particles are perpendicular ⊥ to the direction of travel of the wave. It has crests and troughs.
- **Longitudinal wave:-** In it the vibrations of particles are parallel to the direction of travel of wave. It has compressions and rarefactions.
- **Echo:** The repetition of sound due to reflection of sound waves, is called an **echo.**
- **Sonar:** It stands for **sound navigation** and **ranging**. It is used to measure the depth of a sea to locate the enemy submarines and shipwrecks.

Anatomy of an Electromagnetic Wave

- **Mechanical waves and electro-magnetic waves** are two important ways through which energy is transported in the world around us.
- Waves in water and sound waves in air are two examples of **mechanical waves.**
- **Electromagnetic waves** do not require a medium to propagate.
  Examples are light, radio waves, X-rays etc.
- **Sound waves** cannot travel in the vacuum because there is no medium to transmit these mechanical waves.
- **Sound** is transmitted through gases, plasma, and liquids as longitudinal waves, also called **compression waves.**
- Audible sound for human is from **20 Hz** to about **20000 Hz.**
- **Pitch** is the property of sound that we perceive as higher and lower tones.
- Sounds higher than **20000 Hz** are called **ultrasonics.**
- Sounds less than 20 Hz are called **infrasonics.**
- When temperature is increased the speed of sound is increased.
- Speed of sound in air is 330 m/s.

Speed of Sound in Different Mediums

Medium	Speed of sound (In m/s)
Air(0°C)	332
Air (20°C)	343
Iron	5130
Glass	5640

Light

- **Light** is a form of energy which produces sensation of vision on our eyes.
- Light is made of discrete packets of energy called **photons.**
- **Photons** carry momentum, have no mass, and travel at the speed of light, i.e. **300,000 km/sec.**
- Sun's light reaches to earth in 8 **minutes** 19 seconds (i.e. 499 seconds).
- The light reflected from moon reaches to earth in **1.28** second.

Transparent, Translucent and Opaque Matter

Matter	Nature	Example
Transparent	It allows most of light to pass through.	glass, water, etc
Translucent	It allows a part of light falling on it to pass through.	oiled paper
Opaque	It does not allow the incident light to pass through.	mirror, metal, wood, etc.

- **Ultraviolet radiation** is an electromagnetic radiation that has wavelength from 400 nm to 10 nm, shorter than that of visible light but longer than X-rays. It is used in water purification.
- **Infrared radiation** is emission of energy as electromagnetic waves in the portion of the spectrum just beyond the limit of the red portion of visible radiation.
- **X-rays** are electromagnetic radiation having a shorter wavelength and produced by bombarding a target made of tungsten, with high speed electrons. Uses in medical diagonosis.
- **Microwaves** are short, high frequency waves lying roughly between very high frequency (infrared) waves and conventional radio waves.

Reflection of light

Reflection by Plane Mirror The image formed by the plane mirror is always erect, of the same size and at the same distance as the object is.

Spherical mirror

Spherical mirrors are of two types
(i) Concave mirror
(ii) Convex mirror

Position & Nature of image formed by a Spherical Mirror

Position of object	Position of image	Size of image in comparison to object	Nature of image
Concave mirror			
At infinity	At focus	Highly diminished	Real, inverted
Between infinity and centre of curvature	Between focus and centre of curvature	Diminished	Real, inverted
At centre of curvature	At centre of curvature	Of same size	Real, inverted
Between focus and centre of curvature	Between centre of curvature and infinity	Enlarged	Real, inverted
At focus	At infinity	Highly enlarged	Real, inverted
Between focus and pole	Behind the mirror	Enlarged	Virtual, erect
Convex mirror			
At infinity	At Focus	Highly diminished	Virtual, erect
Infront of mirror	Between pole and focus	Diminished	Virtual, erect

Uses of Concave Mirror

(i)   As a shaving mirror.
(ii) As a reflector for the head lights of a vehicle, search light.
(iii) In opthalmoscope to examine eye, ear, nose by doctors.
(iv) In solar cookers,

Uses of Convex Mirror

(i)   As a rear view mirror in vehicle because it provides the maximum rear field of view and image formed is always erect.
(ii) In sodium reflector lamp.

Refraction of Light

The bending of the light ray from its path in passing from one medium to the other medium is called refraction of light.

- If the refracted ray bends towards the normal relative to the incident ray, then the second medium is said to be **denser** than the first medium. But if the refracted ray bends away from the normal, then the second medium is said to be **rarer** than the first medium.

Some Phenomena based on Refraction

(i)   **Twinkling** of stars
(ii) **Oval Shape** of sun in the morning and evening.
(iii) Rivers appear **shallow**
(iv) Coins appear **raised** in glass filled with water.
(v)   Pencils appear **broken** in the beaker filled with water.
(vi) Sun appears **above horizon** at sunset and sunrise.

Total Internal Reflection

When the angle of incidence, for a ray of light passing from a denser medium to a rarer medium, exceeds a particular value (called **critical angle** for which angle of refraction 90°), the ray reflects back in the same medium from the boundary. This phenomena is called **total internal reflection.**

Some Phenomena of total Internal Reflection

(i)   Endoscopy using optical fibre.
(ii) Sparkling of diamond.
(iii) Mirage in desert
(iv) Increase in duration of sun's visibility.
(v)   Appearance of air bubbles in glass paper weight.
(vi) Shining of air bubbles in water.

Scattering of Light: Sunlight gets scattered by small particles present in the atmosphere. **Red** colour scatters least and violet most. Some phenomena like – **reddish** appearance of the sun at **sunrise** and **sunset, blue colour** of sky, white colour of clouds etc. based on scattering of light.

Human Eye

The normal range of vision for a healthy human eye is from 25 cm (least distance of distinct vision to infinity (far point).

Defects of Vision & Remedies

Myopia or Near(short) sightedness

- A person suffering from Myopia can't see the far (distant) object clearly but can see nearby object clearly.

Causes

- The eye ball is too long (i.e. elongated) so image is formed before retina.
- Lens being too curved for the length of the eye ball.

Remedy: Concave lens is used to diverge the rays at retina.

Hyperopia or Hypermetropia (long (far) sightedness)

- A person suffering from it can't see near object clearly but can see distant object clearly.

Causes

- The eye ball is too short so image is formed beyond the retina.
- Cornea is not curved enough,
- Eye lens is farther back in the eye.

Remedy: Convex lens is used to converge the rays at retina.

Target group: It can affects both children and adults.

Astigmatism

Astigmatism is the most common refractive problem responsible for **blurry vision. Cylindrical** lens is used to correct astigmatism.

Cataract

- It is the clouding of the lens of the eye that prevent a person to see.
  Causes: Protein builds up in the eye lens & make it cloudy.

Remedy:

- It can be corrected with suitable eye glasses (lenses).
- Cataract surgery is performed when eye glass does not suit.

Dispersion of Light

The splitting of white ray of light into its seven constituents colours (VIBGYOR) is called **dispersion of light**.

* The band of seven constituents colours is called **spectrum**.

Microscope: It is used to see magnified image of a tiny objects.

Telescope: It is used to increase the visual angle of distant object. It is used to see far off objects clearly.

Electricity

* **Electricity** is the set of physical phenomena associated with the presence and flow of electric charge.
* **Electric charge** is a property of some sub-atomic particles, which determines their electromagnetic interactions.
  The **SI unit** of charge is **coulomb** (c).

Electric Current (I)

It is a movement or flow of electrically charged particle per unit time.

* Electrical currents generate magnetic fields, and changing magnetic fields generate electrical currents.

Conductors

These are the substances which allow the passage of electric charge with low resistance. E.g., silver, copper etc.

Silver is the best conductor of electricity followed by **copper.**

Insulators

These are substances which do not allow passage of electric charge, e.g. rubber, wood, mica, glass, ebonite etc.

* The **resistance** is the obstruction offered to the flow of electric current.

Electric Cell

It is the device used to convert chemical energy into electrical energy.

* **Ammeter**- Measures current
* **Voltmeter**- Measures the potential difference between two points in a circuit.
* **Fuse** is a safety device that protects an electric circuit from becoming overloaded.

Transformer

* Transformer is a device which converts low voltage AC into high voltage Ac and vice-versa.

Application /uses: As voltage regulators for –
(i) T.V, refrigerator, computer, air conditioner, etc.

(ii) Induction furnaces.
(iii) for welding purposes.

AC Generator/Dynamo/Alternator

* It is an electric device used to convert mechanical energy into electrical energy.

D.C. Motor

* It converts direct current energy from a battery into mechanical energy of rotation.
* **Its uses**
(i) In D.C. fans, exhaust, ceiling, table fans, etc.
(ii) In pumping water.
(iii) In running tram-cars, trains, etc.

Magnetism

Magnets : The material or body which attract magnetic substance like iron, cobalt, nickel, etc.

* The force of attraction of a magnet is **greater at its poles than in the middle.**
* **Similar** poles of two magnets repel each other.
* Opposite poles of two magnets attract each other.
* If a **bar magnet** is suspended by a thread and free to rotate, its South Pole will move towards the North Pole of the earth and vice versa.

Uses/Applications

* Magnets are used in making magnetic compasses which help **sailors** and **navigators** to know the **directions.**
* **Electromagnets** are used in generators, motors, loud speakers, telephones, TV sets, fans, mixers, electric bells, Maglev etc.

Modern Physics

* The nucleus of an atom consists of protons and neutrons together called nucleons.

X-Rays

X-rays are electromagnetic radiations of very short wavelength (0.1 Å to 100 Å) and high energy which are emitted when fast moving electrons or cathode rays strike a target of high atomic mass.

Properties of X-Rays

(i) These are highly **penetrating rays** and can pass through several materials which are opaque to ordinary light.
(ii) They affect **photographic plates.**

Nuclear Fission: The process of splitting of a heavy nucleus into two nuclei of comparable size and release of large energy is called **fission, eg. atom bomb.**

- **Nuclear Fusion :** The process in which two or more lighter nuclei combine to form a heavy nucleus is known as nuclear fusion, e.g. hydrogen bomb.

Important Discoveries in Physics

Discovery	Scientist	Year
Atom	John Dalton	1808
Photography (On paper)	W.Fox Talbot	1835
Dynamite	Alfred Nobel	1867
X-Rays	Roentgen	1895
Electron	J.J. Thomson	1897
Radium	Madam Curie	1898
Wireless telegram	Marconi	1901
Proton	Goldstein	1886
Raman effect	C.V. Raman	1928
Neutron	James Chadwick	1932

Significant Inventions

Invention	Inventor	Country	Year
Aeroplane	Wright brothers	USA	1903
Barometer	E. Torricelli	Italy	1644
Bicycle	K. Macmillan	Scotland	1839
Calculating machine	Pascal	France	1642
Centrigrade scale	A. Celsius	France	1742
Diesel engine	Rudolf Diesel	Germany	1892
Dynamo	Michael Faraday	England	1831
Electric lamp	Thomas Alva Edison	USA	1879
Fountain Pen	L.E. Waterman	USA	1884
Jet Engine	Sir Frank Whittle	England	1937
Lift	E.G. Otis	USA	1852
Match (safety)	J.E. Lundstrom	Sweden	1855
Microphone	David Hughes	USA	1878
Motor car(petrol)	Karl Benz	Germany	1885
Motorcycle	Edward Butler	England	1884
Printing Press	J. Gutenberg	Germany	1455
Radio	G.Marconi	England	1901
Razor (safety)	K.G. Gillette USA	USA	1895
Refrigerator	J. Harrison and A. Catlin	Britain	1834
Steam engine (condenser)	James Watt	Scotland	1765
Telephone	Alexander Graham Bell	USA	1876
Television	John Logie Bared	Scotland	1926
Thermometer	Galileo Galilei	Italy	1593

CHEMISTRY

- **Chemistry** is the branch of science which deals with study of matter and various changes it undergoes.

Classification of Matter

Matter

- It is defined as anything that occupies space and has mass.
- At a given temperature, an element is in one of the three states of matter- **Solid, Liquid** or **Vapour** (Gas).

Solids

- Solids possess definite shape and volume, eg. metals, brick, etc.

Liquids

- They possess definite volume but no definite shape.
- They can flow, so they are called fluids, e.g. water, milk, mercury, oil,etc.

Gases

- Gases have neither a definite volume nor definite shape.
- They takes the volume and shape of the container. E.g.– air, oxygen, hydrogen, etc.
- **Melting point** of a substance is the temperature at which its solid form changes to a liquid.
- **Boiling point** is the temperature at which the liquid form of a substance changes to a gas.
- A **physical change** is a change in matter that involves no chemical reaction.
- The three types of physical changes are- **melting, evaporation** and **freezing**.
- **Chemical Change:** A change in which the identify of the original substance is changed and new substances are formed is called a chemical change for example souring of milk, burning of paper, rusting of iron etc.

Atom

- An **atom** is the **smallest unit** of an element.
- An atom has a central **nucleus.**
- The nucleus carries a **positive charge**.
- Electrons revolves around the nucleus.
- **Protons** have a **positive** charge.
- **Electrons** have a **negative** charge.
- **Neutrons** have **no charge**.

Element

- Everything in the universe is made of a combination of a few basic substances called **elements.**
- The element is the simplest form of matter composed of atoms having identical number of protons in each nucleus.

Compound

- A **compound** is a pure substance that contains atoms of two or more chemical elements in definite proportions that cannot be separated by physical means and are held together by chemical bonds.

Air and Water

Air is colorless, odorless, tasteless, gaseous mixture, mainly contains nitrogen (approximately 78%) and oxygen (approximately 21%) with lesser amounts of argon, carbon dioxide, hydrogen, neon, helium, and other gases.

- **Water** consists of hydrogen and oxygen in the ratio of 2:1 by volume and 1:8 by mass. eg. (H_2O)
- **Hard water** has bicarbonates, chlorides sulphates of Ca and Mg. This water is unfit for washing and use in industrial boilers.
- **Heavy water** is **deuterium oxide** (D_2O), molecular mass = 20).

Substances & Chemical Compositions

Common Name	Chemical Name	Composition	Formula
Alum	Potash	Potassium, Sulphur, Aluminium, Hydrogen and Oxygen	$K_2SO_4Al_2(SO_4)_3$
Bleaching Powder	Calcium hypochlorite	Calcium, Chlorine and Oxygen	$CaCl(OCl)$

Blue Vitriol	Copper sulphate	Copper, Sulphur and Oxygen	$CuSO_4.5H_2O$
Caustic Potash	Potassium hydroxide	Potassium Hydrogen, and Oxygen	KOH
Chalk	Calcium carbonate	Calcium, Carbon and Oxygen	$CaCO_3$
Caustic Soda	Sodium hydroxide	Sodium, Hydrogen and Oxygen	NaOH
Baking Soda	Sodium bicarbonate	Sodium, Hydrogen, Carbon and Oxygen	$NaHCO_3$
Common Salt	Sodium chloride	Sodium and Chlorine	NaCl
Galena	Lead sulphide	Lead and Sulphur	PbS
Green Vitriol	Iron sulphate	Iron, Sulphur and Oxygen	$FeSO_4. 7H_2O$
Glauber's salt Gypsum	Sodium sulphate Calcium Sulphate dihydrate	Sodium, Sulphur, Oxygen and hydrogen	$Na_2SO_4.10H_2O$ $CaSO_4.2H_2O$
Laughing gas	Nitrous oxide	Nitrogen and Oxygen	N_2O
Lime water	Calcium hydroxide	Calcium, Hydrogen, and Oxygen	$Ca(OH)_2$
Plaster of Paris	Calcium sulphate hemihydrate	Calcium, Sulphur, Hydrogen and Oxygen	$2CaSO_4.H_2O$
Quick lime	Calcium oxide	Calcium and Oxygen	CaO
Red lead	Triplumbic	Lead and Oxygen	Pb_3O_4
Soda ash or washing soda	Sodium carbonate	Sodium, Carbon, Hydrogen and Oxygen	$Na_2CO_3.10H_2O$
Soda bicarbonate	Sodium bicarbonate	Sodium hydrogen, Carbon and Oxygen	$NaHCO_3$
White vitriol	Zinc sulphate	Zinc, Sulphur, Hydrogen and Oxygen	$ZnSO_4.7H_2O$

Metals and Non-Metals

- There are two types of elements- metals and non- metals.

Metals

- Elements which are hard, ductile, brittle, and malleable, possess lustre and conduct heat and electricity are termed **metals.**
- Except **Mercury and gallium**, all metals are solid.

Non-Metals

- Non metals are electronegative elements which have a tendency to gain one or more electrons to form negative ions called **anions.**
- Non metals are **non lustrous** and bad conductors of heat and electricity.

Uses of Metals and Non-Metals Compounds

- **Silver Nitrate** ($AgNO_3$) is called lunar caustic and is used to prepare the ink used during voting.
- **Hydrogen Peroxide** (H_2O_2) is used as an oxidishing agent, bleaching agent, as an insecticide and for washing old oil paintings.
- **Ferric Oxide** (Fe_2O_3) is used in jeweller's rouge.
- **Silver Iodide** (AgI) is used for artificial rain.

Fuels

- The substance, which produce heat and light on combustion are called **fuels.**

- **LPG** (Liquified petroleum gas) is a mixture of hydrocarbons containing three or four carbon atoms, such as propane, butane and pentane.

Coal

- Coal is made up of **carbon.**
- The common varieties of coal are **anthracite, bitumen; lignite** and **peat.**

Acids, bases and pH Scale

Acids

These are chemical compounds that **taste sour**, turn blue litmus red, and often react with some metals to produce hydrogen gas.
- Acids- HNO_3, HNO_2, H_2SO_4, H_3PO_4, H_3PO_3, H_2CO_3, etc.

Bases

These are chemical compounds that **taste bitter**, turn red litmus blue and feel **slippery**.
Base: $(NaOH)$, $(Ca(OH)_2)$, (KOH), $(RbOH)$, etc.
- When aqueous (water) solutions of an acid and a base are combined, a neutralization reaction occurs.
- The **pH** of a solution measures the hydrogen ion concentration in that solution.
- Anything above pH 7 is alkaline, anything below pH 7 is considered acidic.
- Human blood pH should be slightly alkaline (7.35-7.45).

Sources of Some Naturally Occurring Acids

Acid	Source
Citric acid	Lemon, orange, grapes
Maleic acid	Unripe apple
Tartaric acid	Tamarind
Acetic acid	Vinegar
Lactic acid	Milk
Hydrochloric acid	Stomach
Oxalic acid	Tomato

pH Value of Substances

Sodium Hydroxide: Alkaline	14.0
Ammonia	11.0
Baking Soda	8.3
Human Blood	7.35 to 7.45
Pure Water: Neutral	7.0
Milk: Acid	6.6
Tomatoes	4.5
Wine and Beer	4.0
Apples	3.0
Vinegar	2.2
Lemon Juice	2.0
Battery Acid	1.0
Urine(Human)	5.5 to 7.5
Tears	7.4
Sea water	8.5
Milk (Cow)	6.3 to 6.6
Coffee	5.0
Tooth paste	9.0

Plastics and Polymers

- **Plastics** consist of very long molecules, each composed of carbon atoms linked into chains.
- **Polythene** is composed of over 200000 carbon atoms.
- **Polymers** are large long chain like molecules formed by the chemical linking of many smaller molecules.

Radioactivity

- **Radioactivity** is discovered by French physicist **Henry de Becquerel** in 1896, who observed that uranium mineral gave off invisible radiation.
- Radiations are of three kinds: Alpha, Beta and Gamma
- Alpha (α) Particle is **positively charged helium atom** that has very little penetrating power.
- **Beta (β) Particles** are negatively charged light particles.
- **Gamma (γ) Particles** are **electromagnetic radiations** of low wavelength, high frequency, and high energy.

Electroplating

- It is a process of plating one metal onto another by **electrolysis**, most commonly for **decorative purposes** or to prevent **corrosion** of a metal.
- **Types of electroplating** capsopper plating, silver plating, and chromium plating, etc.

Carbon and Its Compounds

- All organic compounds contain carbon, and the vast majority also contains hydrogen bonded to carbon.
- It is non-metal.
- Its atomic number is 6 & mass is 12.

Allotropes

- Allotropes are substances which have same chemical properties but different physical properties.

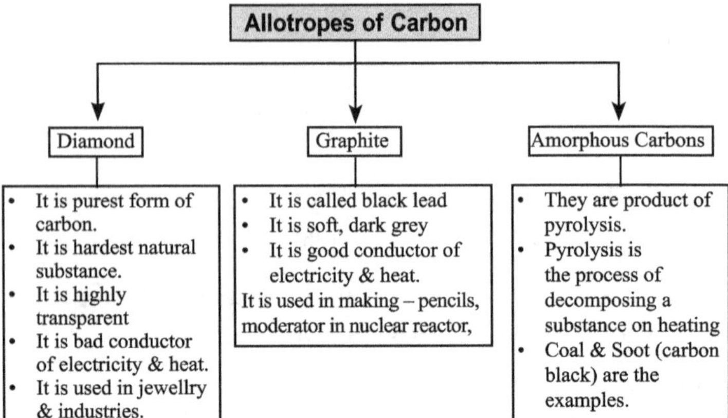

Glass

Glass is a mixture of an alkali silicate with the silicate of a base, that is, silica, sodium silicate and calcium or lead silicate.

Type & Uses

(i) **Milky Glass** is used to the melt glass.

(ii) **Flint Glass,** used in lenses, prisms.

(iii) **Soda or Soft Glass** is used for making bottles, window panes, etc.

(iv) **Potash Glass or Hard Glass** is used for making beakers, flasks, funnel, etc.

(v) **Crown Glass** is used for **optical** apparatus.

(vi) **Crook's Glass** is used for **spectacles** as it absorbs UV rays.

(vii) **Glass Laminates** is used to make windows and screens of cars, trains and aircraft.

(viii) **Jena Glass** is used for making laboratory bottles, for keeping acids and alkalies.

Chemical Substances

Soaps and Detergents: Soaps are the sodium or potassium salts of fatty acids.

Antibiotic: Medicinal compounds produced by moulds and bacteria, capable of destroying or preventing the growth of bacteria in animal systems. For example penicillin, chloramphenicol etc.

Antipyretic: A substance used to lower body temperature.

Sulphadrugs: Alternatives of antibiotics, sulphanilamide, sulphadiazine, Sulpha gunamidine.

Antacids: Substances which neutralise the excess acid and raise the pH to appropriate level in stomach are called antacids.

Saccharin: A white crystalline solid which is 550 times sweeter than sugar, but does not have any food value. It is used by diabetic patients.

DDT: Dichloro diphenyl tricholoro ethane, a white powder used as an insecticide.

Fertilizers

Fertilizers are chemical compounds which when added to the soil increase their fertility and directly supply the need of essential elements [N, P, K] of primary importance.

Classification

Chemical fertilizers are broadly classified into the following three types:

(i) **Nitrogenous fertilizers:** Ammonium sulphate, urea etc.

(ii) **Phosphatic fertilizers:** Super phosphate, ammonium phosphate

(iii) **Potash fertilizers:** Potassium chloride, potassium sulphate.

Soaps and Detergents

Soap: Fatty acid salts of sodium and potassium are known as soaps. These are prepared by the action of fatty acids with sodium hydroxide or potassium hydroxide.

Fatty acid + sodium hydroxide

$\rightarrow$ Soap + glycerol.

Detergents are sodium salt of long chain sulphonic acids or alkyl hydrogen sulphate.

Advantages of detergents over soaps

(i) Detergents can be used for laundering even with hard water as they are soluble even in hard water.

(ii) Detergents possess better cleansing properties than soaps.

Disadvantages of detergents over soap: Detergents are prepared from hydrocarbons, while soaps are prepared from edible fatty oils. Thus they are non biodegradable.

Saponification

It is the process of making of soap by the hydrolysis of fats and oils with alkalis.

Both soaps and detergents are soluble in water and act as surfactants which reduce the surface tension of water to a great extent.

Branches of Science

Branch		Study
Arthrology	–	study of joints
Carpology	–	study of fruits and seeds
Cosmology	–	study of the universe
Dactylography	–	the study of fingerprints
Ecology	–	study of environment
Endocrinology	–	study of ductless glands
Entomology	–	study of insects
Geology	–	study of earth's crust
Hematology	–	study of blood
Hepatology	–	study of liver
Herpetology	–	study of reptiles and amphibians
Hypnology	–	study of sleep; study of hypnosis
Ichthyology	–	study of fish
Laryngology	–	study of larynx
Mastology	–	study of mammals or mammary glands or breast diseases
Meteorology	–	study of weather
Neonatology	–	study of newborn babies
Nephrology	–	study of the kidneys
Odontology	–	study of teeth
Oncology	–	study of tumours
Pathology	–	study of disease
Pharmacology	–	study of drugs
Physiology	–	study of processes of life
Pyretology	–	study of fevers
Radiology	–	study of X-rays and their medical applications.
Seismology	–	study of earthquakes
Urology	–	study of urine; urinary tract
Virology	–	study of viruses
Zoiatrics	–	veterinary surgery
Zoology	–	study of animals

BIOLOGY

Introduction

Biology is the study of life and living organism, including their structure, function, evolution, distribution, identification and Taxonomy

- **Aristotle** is often called "the father of biology".
- **Leeuwenhoek** invented a simple microscope and studied living cells.
- **Gregor Johann Mendel** discovered principles of inheritance.
- **Robert Hooke** assembled a compound microscope and discovered cells in cork.
- **Charles Darwin** is famous for the theory of Natural selection.
- **Hippocrates** is considered to be the *"father of western medicine"*.
- **Edward Jenner** is famous for creating the first effective vaccine for smallpox- (*father of immunology*)
- **William Watson (1909)** introduced the term Genetics.
- **Watson and Crick** gave the model of DNA.
- **In 1866 Ernst Haeckel** coined word "ecology"
- **Camillo golgi** discovered golgi body.
- **Salim Ali** known as the *"birdman of India"*
- **Har Gobind Khorana** is a biochemist who won the Nobel Prize in 1968 for demonstrating how the *nucleotides in nucleic acids control the synthesis of proteins.*

Cells

- All living organism are constituted of structural and functional units called cells.
- *Robert Hook* coined the term '*cell*' in 1665.
- Cells are grouped into tissues, tissues into organ and organs into organ system.
- Smallest cells- Mycoplasmas.
- Largest isolated single cell- egg of an ostrich
- Prokaryotic is without nucleus. It is found in bacteria, blue green algae, mycoplasma.
- The **eukaryotic cells** with nucleus occur in all protists, fungi, plants and the animals.

- **Cell wall** is present in plants cell.
- **Cell membrane** is composed of lipids.
- The function of plasma membrane is the transport of the molecules across it.
- **Ribosomes** were first observed by *Palade*.
- Ribosomes are present only in grandular endoplasmic reticulum.
- Except mammalian RBC all living cells have ribosomes.
- **Nucleus** is centrally located spherical and largest component of all eukaryotic cell. **Nucleolus** is present in nucleus.
- **Mitochondria** are also called *"Powerhouse of cells"*. They are involved in energy generation.

Genetics

- Study of genes is known as **genetics**.
- Gene is a segment of DNA and *basic unit of heredity.* These are located on chromosomes.
- **DNA** is found in nucleus, and also found in mitochondria and chloroplast.
- It stands for **deoxyribonucleic acid (DNA).**
- It is double stranded.
- It consists of Nitrogenous bases-**Adenine, Thymine, Cytosine** or **Guanine**, 5-carbon sugar and a phosphate molecule.
- **RNA** is single stranded. It consists of phosphate, ribose sugar, nitrogenous bases- **Adinine, Uracil, Cytosine**, and **Guanine**.
- **Mendel** conducted cross hybridization experiments on green pea plant (*Pisum sativum*).

Mutation : Sudden change in the sequence of DNA is known as mutation.

Sex Determination

- X and Y are the sex chromosomes which are responsible for the determination of sex. 46 chromosomes are present in human body cell. In which 22 pairs of these are *autosomes* & 23rd is sex chromosomes, ie. *x & y.*

Digestion of Food

Name of the Digestive juice	Name of the enzymes	Substrate	End product
Saliva	Ptyalin (Salivary amylase)	Starch	Maltose
Pancreatic juice	Amylopsin (pancreatic amylase)	Starch, Glycogen	Maltose and Glucose
Intestinal juice	Sucrase (invertase), Maltase, Lactase	Sucrose; Maltose, Lactose	Glucose and fructose, Glucose, and galactose
Gastric Juice	Pepsin, Rennin	Proteins, Casein	Proteoses and peptones, Calcium caseinate
Pancreatic Juice	Trypsin, Chymotrypsin, Carboxyl peptidases	Proteins, Peptides	Proteoses and Peptides Amino acid.
Intestinal juice	Amino peptidase, Dipeptidase	Peptides	Amino acids

Vitamin Required by the Body

Vitamin	Chemical Name	Function in Body	Deficiency Disease	Sources
B_1	Thiamine pyrophosphate	Part of coenzyme for respiration	**Beri-beri:** nerve and heart disorders	Found in whole grain cereals, etc.
B_2	Riboflavin	Part of coenzyme FAD needed for respiration	**Ariboflavinosis:** skin and eye disorders	Milk, yogurt, etc.
B_{12}	Cyanoco-balamin	Coenzyme needed for making red blood cells, etc.	**Pernicious anaemia**	Animal products etc.
B_5	Nicotinic acid ('niacin')	Part of coenzymes NAD, NADP used in respiration	**Pellagra:** skin, gut and nerve disorders	Widespread in foods.
C	Ascorbic acid	Not precisely known	**Scurvy:** degeneration of skin teeth and blood vessels.	Lemon, orange, etc.
A	Retinol	Visual pigment, rhodopsin	**Xeropthalmia:** 'dry eyes'	Milk, eggs, etc.
D	Cholecalciferol	Stimulates calcium absorption by small intestine, needed for proper bone growth	**Rickets:** bone deformity	Found in dairy products, etc.
E	Tocopherol	Not precisely known	**Infertility**	Found primarily in plant oils, green, leafy vegetables, etc.
K	Phylloquinone	Involved in blood clotting	**Possible haemorrage**	Green, leafy vegetables, etc.

Minerals Required by the Body

Minerals	Source	Function
Sodium (Na)	Table salt large amounts is present in processed foods, etc.	for proper fluid balance, etc.
Chloride	Table salt, large amounts is present in processed foods, etc.	for proper fluid balance, etc.
Potassium	Meats, milk, etc.	for proper fluid balance, etc.
Calcium	Milk and milk products, etc.	Important for healthy bones and teeth, etc.
Phosphorus	Meat, fish, poultry, eggs, milk, processed foods.	Important for healthy bones and teeth, etc.
Magnesium	Nuts and seeds; etc.	Found in bones, etc.
Sulfur	Occurs in foods as part of protein, meats, etc.	Found in protein molecules.
Iron	Organ meats; etc.	found in red blood cells.
Iodine	Seafood, foods grown in iodine-rich soil, etc.	Found in thyroid hormone.

Protein Deficiency Diseases

- **Marasmus** is produced by a simultaneous deficiency of proteins and calories.
- **Kwashiorkar** is produced by protein deficiency.

Respiratory System

The organ system which aids in the process of respiration is called the Respiratory system.

Organs of Respiration in Animals

Respiratory Organ	Animals
Lungs	Mammals, Birds, Reptiles and Amphibians
Gills	Fish, Crabs, Tadpole larva of Frog
Skin	Earthworm, Leech, Amphibians
Trachea	Insects

Human Respiratory System

- Human respiratory system consists of external nostrils, nasal cavity, nasopharynx, larynx, trachea, bronchiole and lungs.

Circulatory System

- These are of two types open circulatory system and closed circulatory system.
- Closed present in arthopods and molluscs.
- Annelids and chordates have a closed circulatory.
- The human heart beats at the rate of about 72-80 times per minute in the resting condition.
- ECG stands for Electrocardiogram. It is the graphic record of electronic current produced by the excitation of cardiac muscles.
- It is process of removal of undigested wastes from the body.
- Kidney plays a major role in the elimination of water waste in the form of urine.
- Urine contains ammonia, urea, uric acid, etc.

Human Skeleton (comprising 206 bones)

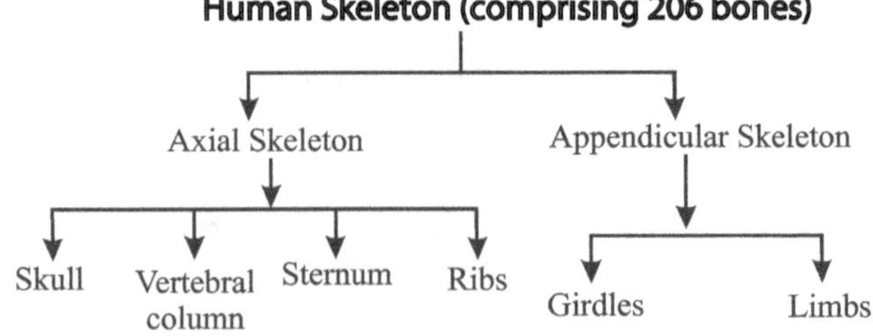

Endocrine System : Hormones and their Action

S. No.	Endocrine gland	Hormone	Action
1	**Pituitary (Master gland)**	Growth hormones, Anti-diuretic hormone Adeno – Corticotrophic hormone	Regulates the growth of bone and tissue. Controls the amount of water reabsorbed by the water. Defending the body against physiological stress e.g. exposure to cold. Follicle stimulating hormone stimulates ovary to produce female hormone.
2	**Pineal**	Melatonin	Regulates, circadian and sexual cycle
3	**Thyroid**	Thyroxine	Regulates rate of growth and metabolism. Too little-over weight and sluggishness. Too much-thin and over active.
4	**Thymus**	Thymosin	Helps in production of lymphocytes
5	**Adrenal**	Cortisone	Aids in conversion of proteins to sugar, cortex of this gland produces the hormone.
6	**Pancreas**	Insulin	Regulates sugar metabolism. Too little insulin leads to high sugar level in blood and weakness (a condition called **diabetes**)
7	**Ovary**	Estrogen	Development of secondary sexual characters e.g. development of breasts in female.
8	**Testis**	Testosterone	Development of many masculine features such as growth of moustaches and beard

Diseases

Common Heart Diseases

- **Coronary artery disease or Arthro-sclerosis :**
- **Angina** (angina pectoris)
- **Heart Failure** (congestive heart failure)

Common Lung Diseases

- **Asthma**
- **Bronchitis (Inflammation of the Bronchi)**

Common Brain Diseases

- **Epilepsy**: Epilepsy is a condition where a person has recurrent seizures, abnormal discharge of electrical activity in the brain cells

Bacteria Diseases

Disease	Pathogen	Affected Organ	Symptom
Anthrax	Bacillus anthracis	Skin and intestine	Skinulcer, sore throat, nausea, fever, breathlessness
Cholera	Vibrio cholerae	Intestine	Vomiting, acute diarrhoea, muscular cramps, dehydration etc.
Diphtheria	Corynebacterium diphtheriae	Respiratory tract	Difficulty In respiration (mainly in child of age 2-5 yrs).
Leprosy or Hansen's disease	Mycobacterium leprae	Chronic infection of skin and nerve	Ulcers, nodules, scaly scabs (the infected part of the body becomes senseless).
Plague (i) Bubonic plague	Pasteurella, Yersinia pestis	Blood disease	High fever, weakness and haemorrhage which turn black.

		Lungs	Haemorrhage of bronchi, lungs.
(ii) Pneumonic plaque		Lungs	Haemorrhage of bronchi, lungs.
Tetanus (lock jaw)	Clostridium tetani	Central nervous system	Painful contraction of neck and jaw muscles followed by paralysis of thoracic muscles.
Tuberculosis	Mycobacterium tuberculosis	Lungs	Repeated coughing, high fever.
Whooping cough or Pertussis	Bacillus pertussis	Respiratory system	Continuous coughing.
Pneumonia	Diplococcus pneumoniae	Lungs	Sudden chill, chest pain, cough, high fever.
Typhoid	Salmonella typhi	intestine	High fever, diarrhoea and headache.

Viral Diseases

Disease	Pathogen	Affected Part	Symptom
AIDS (Acquired Immuno Deficiency Syndrome)	HIV (Human Immuno Deficiency Virus)	White blood cells	Weak immune system.
Chicken pox	Vericella virus	Whole body	High fever, reddish eruption on body
Small pox	Variola virus	Whole body	Light fever, eruption of blood on body
Dengue fever	RNA containing dengue virus	Whole body, particularly head, eyes and joints	High fever, backache, headache, retro-orbital pain behind the eye ball.
Hepatitis (Epidemic Jaundice) (i) Hepatitis - A (ii) Hepatitis - B	Hepatitis virus Hepatitis - A virus Hepatitis - B virus	Liver	Loss of appetite, nausea, whitish stool and jaundice. Not fatal Fatal
Herpes	Herpes virus	Skin	Swelling of skin.
Influenza (flu)	Influenza virus	Whole body	Inflammation of upper respiratory tract, nose throat and eyes.
Measles German	Rubella virus	Whole body	Loss of appetite, reddish eruption on the body.
Polio or poliomyelitis	Polio virus	Throat, backbone and nerve	Fever, backbone and intestine wall cells are destroyed. It leads to paralysis.
Rabies (hydrophobia)	RNA virus called rabies virus	Nervous system	Encephalitis, fear of water, high fever, headache, spasm of throat and chest leading to death
Swine influenza (flu)	H_1N_1 flu virus	Whole body (muscles)	Headache, tiredness, sore throat, vomiting, breathing problems.

Protozoan Diseases

Disease	Pathogen	Vector	Parts Affected
African trypanosomiasis	*Trypanosoma gambienes*	Tsetse fly (Glossina palpalis)	Blood and nervous tissue. Man feels sleepy, may cause death.
Amoebic dysentery (Amoebiasis)	*Entamoeba histolytica*	None, Infection by contamination	Colon (intestine). Develop loose motion with blood, pain in abdomen
Diarrhoea	*Giardia*	None, infection by contamination	Digestive system causes loose motions, vomitting
Filaria or elephantiasis	*Wuchereria bancrofti*	Culex mosquito	Swelling of legs, testes and other body parts.
Kala azar or dum-dum fever	*Leishmania donovani*	Sand flies (Phlebotomus)	Spleen and liver enlarge and high fever develops.
Malaria	*Plasmodium sp.*	Female Anopheles mosquito	Periodical attacks of high fever, pain in joints accompanied by chill, heavy perspiration and fast pulse.

Fungal Diseases in Human Beings

Disease	Pathogen (fungi)	Symptoms
Asthma or aspergillosis	*Aspergillus fumigatus*	Obstruction in the functioning of lungs.
Baldness	*Tinea capitis*	Hair fall
Athlete's foot	*Tinea pedis*	Skin disease, cracking of feet.
Ringworm	*Tricophyton Verrucosum*	Round red spot on skin
Scabies	*Acarus scabiei*	Skin itching and white spot on the skin.

Blood

- **Blood** is a liquid connective tissue.
- Blood has a fluid matrix called plasma.
- **Plasma** is a pale coloured fluid which contributes 55% of blood volume. Plasma contains 90 to 92 % of water.
- Blood corpuscles are of three types: Red blood corpuscles (RBCs) ,white blood corpuscles(WBCs) and Blood platelets.
- RBC's are formed in the red bone-marrow, and lack nucleus.
- **Life span of RBCs** (Erythrocytes) is about 120 days.
- **WBCs (Leueocytes)** are responsible for immunity.
- **WBCs** are manufactured in bone marrow.
- **Neutrophils** and monocytes are phagocytic cells (destroy foreign bodies)
- **Basophils** are involved in inflammatory reactions.
- **Eosinophils** are associated with allergic reactions.
- **Lymphocytes** are responsible for immune response.
- **Platelets** (thrombocytes) are responsible for clotting of blood during accidents.
- For a healthy adult person the average **systolic/diastolic pressure** is 120/80 mm of Hg in arteries near heart.
- **The Rh factor** is a type of protein on the surface of red blood cells. Most people who have the **Rh factor** are **Rh**-positive. Those who do not have the **Rh factor** are **Rh**-negative.

- **Karl Landsteiner** (1900) discovered the blood group in human.
- There are four groups of blood A, B, AB and O.
- **Universal Donor :** *'O'* blood group person can give blood to all the four blood groups (O, A, B, and AB).
- **Universal Recipient :** *'AB'* blood group person can take blood from all the four groups (AB, A, B, O).

Vaccines and Their Doses

Age	Vaccination	Dose
Birth to 12 months	• **DPT** (triple vaccine, against diptheria, whooping cough/pertussis and tetanus) • **Polio** (Sabin's oral, previously Salk's injectible) • **BCG** (Bacillus Calmette Guerin)	• Three doses (commonly oral) at intervals of 4-6 weeks. • Three doses at intervals of 4-6 weeks. • Intradermal and one vaccine
8-24 months	• **DPT** • **Polio** (oral) • **Cholera** vaccine (can be repeated every year before summer)	• Booster dose • Booster dose • One
9-15 months	• **Measles** vaccine (MMR or Measles, Mumps and Rubella)	• one dose
5-6 years	• **DT** (Bivalent vaccine against diphtheria and tetanus) • **TAB** (vaccine against Salmonella typhi, S. paratyphi A and S paratyphi B) or Typhoid Paratyphoid vaccine	• Booster dose • Two doses at intervals of 1-2 months
10 years	• Tetanus, TAB (typhoid)	• Booster dose
16 years	• Tetanus, TAB	• Booster dose

Vaccines and Inventors

Vaccine	Developed by	Country	Year
Small Pox	Edward Jenner	England	1796
Cholera	Louis Pasteur	France	1880
Diphtheria and Tetanus	Emil Adolf Von Behring and Shibasaburo Kitasato	Germany/ Japan	1891
TB Vaccine	Albert Calmette and Camille Guerin	France	1922
Polio Vaccine	Jonas E. Salk	US	1952
Oral Polio Vaccine	Albert Bruce Sabin	US	1955
Measles Vaccine	John F. Enders, Thomas peeble	US	1953
Rabies Vaccine	Louis Pasteur	France	1885
Typhus Vaccine	Charles Nicolle	France	1909
Rubella Vaccine	Paul D.Parkman & Harry M. Meyer jr		1966
Scurvy vaccine	James Lind		1753

Medical Science Discoveries

Invention	Inventor	Year
• Anesthetic	William Morton	1846
• Antiseptic	Joseph Lister (Scotland)	1867
• Artificial heart	Denton Cooley	1969
• Bacteria (discovered)	Anton van Leeuwenhoek	1674
• Contact lenses (glass)	Adolf Fick	1887
• Corneal transplants	Eduard Zirm	1905
• Disposable syringe	Colin Murdoch	1956
• Electrocardiograph	Willem Einthoven	1903
• Gas mask	Garrett Augustus Morgan	1912
• Insulin (discovery)	Frederick Banting and Charles Best	1921
• Pacemaker (human)	Wilson Greatbatch	1960 (first use)
• Pathology	Giovanni Battista Morgagni	1761
• Stethoscope	René Laënnec	1819
• Thermometer (medical)	Thomas Allbutt	1866
• X-rays	Wilhelm Roentgen	1895

Science & Technology

SPACE SCIENCE

ISRO

- Indian Space Research Organisation (ISRO) is the parent agency of Indian space agencies which was established on 15th August 1969.

- The headquarter of this organisation is at Bangalore and it was founded by Vikram Sarabhai with a vision to harness space technology for national development.

Indian Space Programme At a Glance				
Satellite	**Date**	**Launch Vehicle**	**Place**	**Remarks**
Aryabhatta	19th April, 1975	Cosmos	Baikonur	Experimental
Bhaskara I	7th June, 1979	Cosmos	Baikonur	Earth Observation
Rohini	10th August, 1979	S L V-3	Sriharikota	Experimental
Apple	19th June, 1981	Ariane	Kourou	Communication
INSAT-IA	10th April, 1982	Delta	America	Communication
Ocean Sat-1 or IRS P4	26th May, 1999	PSLV-C2	Sriharikota	Earth Observation
INSAT-3B	22nd March, 2000	Ariane-5	Kourou	Communication
GSAT-1	18th April, 2001	GSLV-D1	Sriharikota	Communication
INSAT-3A	10th April, 2003	Ariane-5	Kourou	Communication
GSAT-2	8th May, 2003	GSLV-D2	Sriharikota	Communication
EDUSAT	20th September, 2004	GSLV-F01	Sriharikota	Communication
CARTOSAT 1	5th May, 2005	PSLV-C6	Sriharikota	Earth Observation
CHANDRA-YAAN-1	22nd October, 2008	PSLV-C11	Sriharikota	Moon Mission
OCEANSAT-2	23rd September, 2009	PSLV-C14	Sriharikota	Earth Observation
YOUTHSAT	20th April, 2011	PSLV-C16	Sriharikota	Experimental/Small Satellite
RESOURCESAT-2	20th April, 2011	PSLV-C16	Sriharikota	Earth Observation Satellite
GSAT-8	21st May, 2011	Ariane-5 VA-202	Kourou	Communication
GSAT-12	15th July, 2011	PSLV-C17	Sriharikota	Communication
IRNSS-1A	1st July, 2013	PSLV-C22	Sriharikota	Navigation Satellite
GSAT-7	30th August, 2013	Ariane-5 VA-215	Kourou	Communication

MOM	5th November, 2013	PSLV-C25	Sriharikota	Geo-Stationary Satellite
IRNSS-IC	16th October, 2014	PSLV-C26	Sriharikota	Navigation
Pratham	26 Sept. 2016	PSLV-C35	Sriharikota	Technology Applications
GSAT-18	6 October 2016	Ariane-5 ECA	Centre Spatial Guyanais, Kourou	Communications
INS-1A (ISRO Nano-Satellite 1A)	15 February 2017	PSLV-C37	Sriharikota	Technology Applications
South Asia Satellite(GSAT-9)	5 May 2017	GSLV Mk.II	Sriharikota	Communications
IRNSS- 1I	12 April 2018	PSLV- C41	Sriharikota	Navigational/Global Positioning
GSAT- 29	14 Nov. 2018	GSLV MK III-D2	Sriharikota	Communications
HYSIS	29 Nov. 2018	PSLV- C43	Sriharikota	Earth Observation Satellite (with hyper spectoral imaging)

Gaganyaan

- Gaganyaan Programme has been approved by the Union cabinet for demonstration of Indian Human Spaceflight capability to low earth orbit for a mission duration ranging from one orbital period to a maximum of seven days.
- Two unmanned flights and one manned flight will be undertaken as part of Gaganyaan Programme.
- A human rated GSLV Mk-lll will be used to carry the orbital module which will have necessary provisions for sustaining a 3-member crew for the duration of the mission.
- First human space flight demonstration is targeted to be completed within 40 months from the date of sanction. Prior to this, two unmanned flights in full complement will be carried out to gain confidence on the technology and mission management aspects.
- The total expenditure will be around 10,000 crore.

DEFENCE & SECURITY

Defence of India

The supreme commander of the Indian Armed Forces is the President of India.

1. Army Command and Headquarters

Command	Headquarters	Command	Headquarters
Western Command	Chandimandir	Eastern Command	Kolkata
Northern Command	Udhampur	Southern Command	Pune
Army Training Comm.	Shimla	Central Command	Lucknow
South Western Comm.	Jaipur		

2. Navy Command and Headquarters:

Command	Headquarters	Command	Headquarters
Eastern Command	Visakhapatnam	Southern Command	Kochi
Western Command	Mumbai		

3. Air Force Command and Headquarters:

Command	Headquarters	Command	Headquarters
Eastern Air Comd.	Shillong	Western Air Comd.	New Delhi
South-West Air Comd.	Gandhinagar	Central Air Comd.	Allahabad
Southern Air Comd.	Thiruvananthapuram		
Maintenance Comd.	Nagpur	Training Comd.	Bangalore

Internal Security of India

Organization	Year	Headquarters
Central Reserve Police Force (CRPF)	1939	New Delhi
National Cadet Corps (NCC)	1948	New Delhi
Indo-Tibetan Border Police (ITBP)	1962	New Delhi
Border Security Force (BSF)	1965	New Delhi
Central Industrial Security Force (CISF)	1969	New Delhi

Defence Training Institutions of India

Institutions	Places
National Defence Academy (NDA)	Khadakwasla (near Pune)
National Defence College (NDC)	New Delhi
Rashtriya Indian Military College (RIMC)	Dehradun
Armed Forces Medical College (AFMC)	Pune
Air Force School	Sambra (Belgaum)
College of Air Warfare	Secunderabad
Air Force Academy	Hyderabad
I.N.S. Chilka	Chilka
I.N.S. Mandovi	Goa
Indian Naval Academy	Ezhimala

INDIA'S MISSILE SYSTEM : AT A GLANCE

S. No.	Missile	Feature	Range
1	Astra Missile	Beyond Visual range **air-to-air** Missile	A range of over 80 km in head on mode and 20 km in tail-chase mode.
2	Shourya Missile	Canisterised **Surface-to-surface** missile	600 km
3	Sagarika Missile (K-15)	**Submarine-to-Surface** Missile	More than 700 km
4	Akash Missile	Medium range **Surface-to-Air** Missile	25 km
5	Nag Missile	Third Generation-fire and forget-**anti-tank** guided missile	4 to 6 km
6	Nirbhay Missile	Long range subsonic **cruise missile**	1000 km

7	Dhanush Missile	The Ship-based **Surface-to-surface** ballistic missile	300 to 350 km
8	BrahMos Missile (Joint Indo-Russia Venture)	Supersonic **cruise missile** (can be launched from ships, submarines, aricrafts and land)	290 km
9	(a) Prithvi-I (Army version)	A single stage liquid-fuelled surface-to-surface missile.	150 km
	(b) Prithivi-II (Air force version)	A single stage liquid-fuelled **surface-to-surface** missile.	250 km
	(c) Prithvi-III (Naval Version)	A two-stage **surface-to-surface** missile (first stage is solid fuelled and second stage is liquid fuelled).	350 km
10	(a) Agni-I	Short range **ballistic missile**	700-800 km
	(b) Agni-II	Medium range **ballistic** missile	2500 km
	(c) Agni-III	Intermediate range **ballistic** missile	3500 km
	(d) Agni-IV	**Intermediate**	4000 km
	(e) Agni-V	Range **ballistic** missile	5500-5800 km
	(f) Agni-VI (tested)	Under development	6000-8000 km

INDIAN SEA-BASED NUCLEAR-ARMED BALLISTIC MISSILES

Name	Type	Maximum range (km)	Status
Dhanush	Short-range	350	Developed and deployed
Sagarika (K-15)	SLBM	700-750 (Approx)	Awaiting deployment on INS
Shaurya (K-4)	SLBM3	3000-3500	Tested

GLOBAL DEFENCE TECHNOLOGIES

Terminal High Altitude Area Defencse (Thaad) System

- Terminal High Altitude Area Defence (THAAD) is a transportable system that intercepts ballistic missiles inside or outside the atomophere during their final, or terminal, phase of flight.
- THAAD uses a one-stage hit-to-kill interceptor to destroy incoming ballistic missile targets.
- The system is able to intercept incoming missiles both inside and just outside of the Earth's atmosphere at a range of 200 kilometers, which mitigates the effects of weapons of mass destruction before they reach the ground.
- This ability to intercept makes THAAD an important part of layered missile defense concepts.

- THAAD was developed by USA after the experience of Iraq's Scud missile attacks during the GULf war in 1991.
- The THAAD interceptor carries no warhead, but relies on its kinetic energy of impact to destroy the incoming missile.
- A kinetic energy hit minimizes the risk of exploding conventional-warhead ballistic missiles, and the warhead of nuclear-tipped ballistic missiles will not detonate on a kinetic-energy hit.

Features of THAAD System

- Interoperable with other ballistic missile defense systems.
- Ability to intercept missile inside and outside the atmosphere.
- Highly mobile and deployable worldwide

RAFALE

Features

- **Crew:** Single/Double
- **Length:** 15.27 m
- **Wingspan:** 10.80 m
- **Height:** 5.34 m
- **Wing area:** 45.7 m^2
- **Empty weight:**
  10,300 kilograms-Rafale-B
  9,850 kilograms - Rafale-C
  10,600 kilograms-Rafale-M
- **Loaded weight:** 15,000 kilograms
- **Max. takeoff weight:** 24,500 kilograms (Type-B/C/D)
- **Fuel capacity:** 4,700 kg (internal for single-seater (Type-C); 4,400 kg for two-seater (Type-B)
- **Powerplant:** 2 × SNECMA M88-2 turbofans
- **Dry thrust:** 50.04 kN each
- **Thrust with afterburner:** 75 kN each

Technical Features

- Rafale is a **twin-jet combat aircraft** manufactured by the French company Dassault Aviation, capable of carrying out a wide range of short and long-range missions, including ground and sea attacks, reconnaissance, high-accuracy strikes and nuclear strike deterrence.
- Initially developed for the French Air Force and Navy. The Rafale entered service with the French Navy in 2004 and the French Air Force in 2006
- It is powered by two **M88-2 engines** (SNECMA), each with a thrust of 75kN.
- The aircraft is equipped for **buddy-buddy** refuelling with a flight refuelling hose reel and drogue pack.
- Rafale has **'Omnirole'** capability to perform several actions at the same time,like can carrying out both air-to-ground as well as air-to-air attacks.
- Rafale can carry six AASM missiles, with each aiming to hit the target with **10m accuracy.**
- It uses **Spectra electronic warfare system** (Thales), which incorporates solid state transmitter technology, a DAL laser warning receiver, missile warning, detection systems and jammers.
- This combat aircraft is equipped with **RBE2 passive electronically scanned radar** (Thales), which has look-down and shoot-down capabilities and can track up to eight targets simultaneously and provides threat identification and prioritisation.
- The aircraft is fitted with an on-board oxygen generation system (OBOGS), which exempt the need for liquid oxygen re-filling or ground support for oxygen production.

ATOMIC & NUCLEAR SCIENCE

Atomic Research

India's atomic research programme is committed to peaceful uses only, for example, atomic power, generation of electricity, development of agriculture and industry, medical science application, etc.

India's journey to atomic energy research started with establishment of the Atomic Energy Commission on 10 August 1948 under the chairmanship of **Dr. Homi J. Bhabha.** Subsequently, DAE was established in 1956 with the following mandate:

(a) To generate safe, economic electrical power from nuclear energy.

(b) To build research reactors and to utilize the radioisotopes produced in these reactors for applications in the field of agriculture and medicine.

(c) To develop advanced technology in areas such as accelerators, lasers, biochemistry, information technology, and materials including development of non-nuclear and strategic materials like titanium.

Nuclear Explosion in India

First-explosion carried out on 18 May 1974 at **Pokhran** in Rajasthan (Thar) desert. Its code name was "**Smiling Buddha**".

Second N. Explosion code name "**Operation**" **Shakti-98** having 5 series Shakti-I, II & III were tested on 11 May, 1998 at 3.43 p.m. and Shakti-IV & V on 13 May at 12.21 p.m. at Pokhran (Rajasthan). **Dr. A.P.J. Kalam** was the Project Leader. He was also scientific advisor to Defence Minister and head of DRDO too.

BARC

Bhabha Atomic Research Centre (BARC) Established in 1957, it is located at **Trombay (Maharashtra),** and is India's largest atomic research centre, for R&D.

BARC's atomic reactors

Aspara: It was commissioned on 4 August 1956. One megawatt swimming pool type reactor produces radio isotopes. It is also the first atomic reactor in Asia.

Cirus (Canada India Reactor): It was shutdown in 2010. Built in 1960, it is a 40 MW reactor and shutdown in 2010.

Zerlina (Zero Energy Reactor for Lattice Investigation and New Assemblies) Commissioned on 14 January 1961, used for studies of uranium heavy water lattice.

Dhruva Commissioned on 15 August 1985, this 100 MW reactor is a completely indigenous nuclear reactor with most advanced laboratories in the world.

Purnima I (Plutonium Reactor for Neutronic Investigation in Multiplying Assemblies) commissioned on 18 May 1972, a plutonium fuelled reactor, shutdown in 1973. It was modified as *Purnima*-II (1984) that used uranium as fuel and it is being further modified as *Purnima*-III (1990).

Kamini: India's first fast breeder neutron reactor, it has been set up at **Kalpakkam (1996)**.

Nuclear Power Plants

Nuclear power is the fourth-largest source of electricity in India after thermal, hydroelectric and renewable sources of electricity. India has 21 nuclear reactors in operation in 7 nuclear power plants, having an installed capacity of 5308 MW and producing a total of 30,292.91 GWh of electricity while seven other reactors are under construction and are expected to generate an additional 6,100 MW.

Power station	Operator	Establishment Date	Location	State
Tarapur Atomic Power Station	NPCIL	1969	Tarapur	Maharashtra
Rajasthan Atomic Power Station	NPCIL	1973	Rawatbhata	Rajasthan
Kakrapar Atomic Power Station	NPCIL	1993	Kakrapar	Gujarat
Kudankulam Nuclear Power Plant	NPCIL	2013	Kudankulam	Tamil Nadu
Kaiga Nuclear Power Plant	NPCIL	2000	Kaiga	Karnataka
Madras Atomic Power Station	NPCIL	1984	Kalpakkam	Tamil Nadu
Narora Atomic Power Station	NPCIL	1991	Narora	Uttar Pradesh
Gorakhpur Atomic Power Station	NPCIL		Fatehabad	Haryana
Talcher Super Thermal Power Station	NTPC	1995	Kaniha	Odisha
Sipat Thermal Power Plant	NTPC	2008	Sipat	Chhattisgarh

Vindhyachal Super Thermal Power Station	NTPC	2013	Singrauli	Madhya Pradesh
Mundra Ultra Mega Power Project	Tata Power	2009	Mundra	Gujarat
Korba Super Thermal Power Plant	NTPC	1983	Jamani Palli	Chhattisgarh
Bhusawal Thermal Power Station	MA-HAGENCO	1968	Deepnagar	Maharashtra
Satpura Thermal Power Station	MPPGCL	1967	Sarni	Madhya Pradesh
Sterlite Jharsuguda Power Station	Vedanta	2006	Jharsuguda	Odisha
Durgapur Thermal Power Station	DVC	1996	Durgapur	West Bengal

Nuclear and Space Research Centres in India

Centres	Places
India Rare Earths Limited	Mumbai
Uranium Corporation of India	Singhbhum
Bhabha Atomic Research Centre (BARC)	Trombay (Mumbai)
Saha Institute of Nuclear Physics	Kolkata
Vikram Sarabhai Space Centre	Thiruvanthapuram
Indian Space Research Organisation (ISRO)	Bangalore
Space Applications Centre	Ahmedabad

Ecology & Environment

Ecology is the branch of biology deals with the relations and interactions between organisms and their environment, including other organisms.

Ecosystem

An ecosystem is a functional unit of nature consisting of abiotic and biotic factors, where the living organisms interact among themselves and also with their physical environment (abiotic factors).

Biodiversity & Wildlife of India

Biodiversity mean diversity of heterogeneity at all levels of biological organisation, i.e from Micro molecules of the cells to the Biomass. The word Biodiversity was popularized by the sociologist Edward Wilson.

As per available data, the varieties of **species** living on the earth are **1753739**. Out of the above species, 134781 are residing in India. **Wild life Institute of India** has divided it into ten biogeographical regions and twenty five biotic provinces.

IUCN at a Glance

- It was founded in **1948** as the world's first global environmental organisation.
- The **IUCN** stands for "The International Union for Conservation of Nature and Natural Resources." Now known as World Conservation Union (WCU).
- The **IUCN Red List** of "Threatened Species" provides taxonomic, conservation status and distribution information on plants, fungi and animals.

Red Data Book

A **Red Data Book** contains lists of species whose continued existence is threatened.
Threatened species on the list, which lists includes;
Indian elephant, Bengal tiger, Indian lion, Indian Rhino, Gaur, lion tailed macaque, Tibetan Antelope, Ganga river dolphin, the Nilgiri Tahr, snow leopard, dhole, black buck, great Indian bustard, forest owlet, white – winged duck and many more are the most endangered animals in India.

CITES

- Convention on International Trade in Endangered species (CITES) was signed in 1975 in Washington.
- Roughly 5,600 species of animals and 30,000 species of plants are protected by CITES against over-exploitation through international trade.

National Biodiversity Authority

The **NBA** is a body corporate established in accordance with the provisions of Sec.8 of the Biological Diversity Act, 2002, at Chennai w.e.f. 1st October 2003. It is an autonomous, statutory and regulatory organization which is intended to implement the provisions of Biological Diversity Act, 2002.

Wetlands

- Wetlands are lands which, due to geological or ecological factors, have a natural supply of water – either from tidal flows, flooding rivers, connections with groundwater, or because they are perched above aquifers.

- The periodicity of water level fluctuations is termed as hydroperiod and it is the key factor that determines the productivity and species composition of the wetland community.

- Generally low lying areas, covered by shallow water and have characteristic soils and water tolerant vegetation.

- Wetlands occupy only 2% of the surface area of earth and they are estimated to contain 10 to 14% of carbon.

- Man made wetlands: paddy fields, fishery ponds, Trapa & Euryale cultivation ponds and other aquaculture habitats.

Biodiversity Conservtion

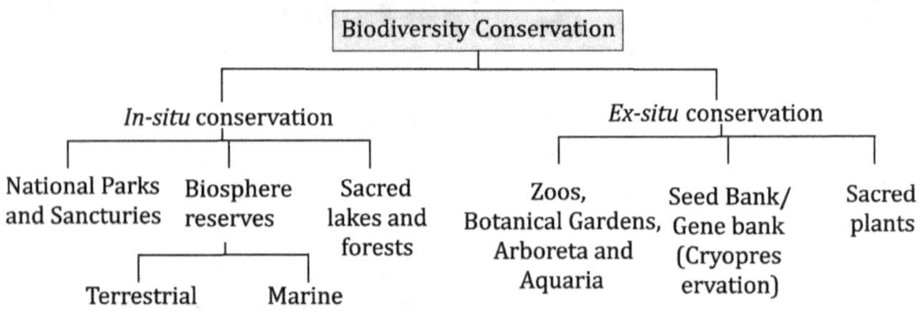

Biosphere Reserves in India

Name	State	Key Fauna
Nilgiri Biosphere Reserve	Tamil Nadu, Kerala and Karnataka	Nilgiri tahr, lion-tailed macaque
Nanda Devi National Park & Biosphere Reserve	Uttarakhand	
Gulf of Mannar	Tamil Nadu	Dugong or sea cow
Nokrek	Meghalaya	Red panda
Sundarbans	West Bengal	Royal Bengal tiger
Manas	Assam	Golden langur, red panda
Simlipal	Odisha	Gaur, royal Bengal tiger, elephant
Dihang-Dibang	Arunachal Pradesh	
Pachmarhi Biosphere Reserve	Madhya Pradesh	Giant squirrel, flying squirrel
Achanakmar-Amarkantak Biosphere Reserve	Madhya Pradesh, Chhattisgarh	Four horned antelope, Indian wild dog, Saras crane)
Great Rann of Kutch	Gujarat	Indian wild ass
Cold Desert	Himachal Pradesh	Snow leopard
Khangchendzonga Biosphere Reserve	Sikkim	Snow leopard, red panda
AgasthyamalI Biosphere Reserve	Kerala, Tamil Nadu	Nilgiri tahr, elephants
Great Nicobar Biosphere Reserve	Andaman and Nicobar Islands	Saltwater crocodile
Dibru-Saikhowa	Assam	Golden langur
Seshachalam Hills	Andhra Pradesh	
Panna	Madhya Pradesh	Tiger, chital, chinkara, sambhar and sloth bear

National Parks

They are reserved for the betterment of wild life, both **fauna and flora.** In national parks private ownership is not allowed. The grazing, cultivation, forestry, etc. is also not permitted. The first national park of the world, **Yellow stone**, in **U.S.A.**, was founded in **1872.**

Important state wise national parks of India		
Jammu and Kashmir	-	Dachigam, Salim Ali
Assam	-	Kaziranga, Manas*
Meghalaya	-	Nokrek
West Bengal	-	Sunderbans
Bihar	-	Hazaribagh, Palamau*
Uttrakhand	-	Corbett* (Hailey), Nanda Devi, Valley of flowers, Rajaji
U. P.	-	Dudhwa*
Gujarat	-	Gir, Marine
Rajasthan	-	Sariska*, Ranthambore*, Desert
Madhya Pradesh	-	Kanha* , Sanjay, Madhav, Panna, Bandhavgarh*, Van Vihar, Fossil
Odisha	-	Simlipal
Karnataka	-	Bandipur*
Kerala	-	Silent Valley, Periyar*
*These national parks are running **Tiger Project** also.		

Sanctuaries

In sanctuaries the protection is given to fauna only. The activity like harvesting of timber, collection of forest products and private ownership rights are permitted so long as they do not interfere with the well being of the animals. The important wild life sanctuaries are: **Chilka wild life sanctuary (Odisha), Bharatpur Bird Sanctuary (Rajasthan), Sultanpur Bird sanctuary (Haryana) and Jalpara sanctuary (West Bengal). Gir wild life sanctuary (Gujarat).**

Pollutants and their Effects

Sr. No.	Pollutant	Origin	Effect
1.	Arsenic (As)	Coal, oil furnaces, glass factories	Lung and skin cancer
2.	Cadmium (Cd)	Smelters, coals, oil furnaces	Damage to lung, kidney, bones
3.	Chlorine (Cl)	Chemical Industries, volcanic activities	Causes irritation
4.	Carbon monoxide (CO)	Motor vehicles, smelters, coal steel plants	Starves body of oxygen, damages heart
5.	Fluoride (F)	Smelters, steel plants	Mottled teeth in children
6.	Formaldehyde (HCHO)	Chemical plants	Allergenic, carcinogenic, headaches, burning sensation in the throat, and can aggravate *asthma symptoms*
7.	HCl (Hydrogen chloride)	Incinerators	Irritates eyes and lungs
8.	Mercury (Hg)	Coal, smelters oil furnaces	Tremors, nerve troubles
9.	Nitric acid (HNO_3)	Formed from NO_2 causes acid rain	Respiratory diseases
10.	Nitrous acid (HNO_3)	Formed from NO_2 and water vapour	Respiratory disease
11.	Hydrogen sulphide (H_2S)	Refineries, Pulp mills	Nausea, irritates eyes

12.	Sulphuric acid (H_2SO_4)	Formed from SO_2 in sunlight with	Respiratory diseases hydroxyl ions
13.	Nitric Oxide (NO)	Motor Vehicles, coal, oil furnaces	Oxidizes to NO_2
14.	Ozone (O_3)	Ground level ozone formed from nitrogen oxides (NO_x) and volatile organic compounds (VOCs)	Asthma, irritates eyes sunlight from nitrogen oxides and hydrocarbons
15.	Lead (Pb)	Motor vehicles, high smelters	Brain damage
16.	Sulfur dioxide (SO_2)	Smelters Coal, Oil furnaces	Irritates eyes, breathing problems

UNFCCC

The United Nations Framework Convention on Climate Change (UNFCCC) entered into force on 21 March 1994. Today, it has near-universal membership. The 195 countries that have ratified the Convention are called **Parties** to the Convention.

Sustainable Development Initiatives of India

- Constitution of the forest conservation act 1980.
- Water (prevention and control of pollution) Act 1974.
- Air(prevention and control of pollution (Act 1981).
- Environment (protection) Act 1986.
- The Wildlife Protection Act ,1972.
- India acceded to the **Vienna convention** for the protection of the ozone layer, March 1985.
- India signed the convention on the **Conservation of Migratory Species of wild animals** (The Bonn Convention) in 1979.
- India signed the **International Convention** for the prevention of pollution of the sea by the oil, 1954(London).

Global Warming/Climate Change

- **Greenhouse Effect-** A greenhouse is an enclosure of glasses in which tropical plants are grown during winters in areas of colder climate. Heat trapped by the glass keeps the temperature inside the greenhouse much higher than the surrounding atmosphere. A similar heating phenomenon occurs in the atmosphere.
- Greenhouse effect is a natural phenomenon which keeps the earth warm at normal level.

Greenhouse Gas	Chemical Formula	Anthropogenic Sources
Carbon dioxide	CO_2	Fossil-fuel combustion, Land-use conversion, Cement Production.
Methane	CH_4	Fossil fuels, Rice paddies, Waste dumps.
Nitrous oxide	N_2O	Fertilizer, Industrial processes, Combustion.
Tropospheric Ozone	O_3	Fossil fuel combustion, Industrial emissions, Chemical solvents.
CFC-12	CCL_2F_2	Liquid coolants, Foams.
HCFC-22	CCl_2F_2	Refrigerants.
Sulfur Hexaflouride	SF_6	Dielectric fluid.

World Wide Fund for Nature

- It was set up in **India in 1969**
- Its coordinating body the **WWF international** is located in Gland in **Switzerland.**
- It has five broad programme components.
- ➤ Promoting India's ecological security,
- ➤ Conserving biological diversity,
- ➤ Ensuring sustainable use of the natural resource base,
- ➤ Minimum pollution,
- ➤ Promoting sustainable lifestyle.

Some of the major environmental Conventions/Protocols

Ramsar Convention, 1971: To prevent the worldwide loss of natural and man-made wetlands through wise use and management of the remaining wetlands.

Montreal Protocol, 1987: To reduce and eventually eliminate the production and consumption of Ozone depleting substances. It considers the fact that the developing countries have hardly had contributed to the problem, so they have a 10 years delay period in phasing out the production and consumption of ozone depleting chemicals over developed nations.

United Nation Framework Convention on Climate Change (UNFCCC), 1992: To provide major framework to regulate anthropogenic climate change.

Rio de Janeiro Earth Summit, 1992: To guide countries in future sustainable development and to prevent environmental degradation. Officially known as United Nations Conference on Environment and Development (UNCED).

Kyoto Protocol, 1997: To mandate country-by-country reductions in greenhouse-gas emissions

Art, Culture & Tourism

Culture plays an important role in the development of any nation. A country as diverse as India is symbolized by the plurality of its culture.

India has one of the world's largest collections of songs, music, dance, theatre, folk traditions, performing arts, rites and rituals, paintings and writings that are known, as the 'Intangible Cultural Heritage' (ICH) of humanity.

Famous Art Forms

Names	State of Origin	Materials Used
Patachitra painting	Raghurajpur Village in Puri district of Odisha	Cloth fortified with tamarind paste, chalk powder and gum and natural dyes.
Bengal pat painting	Bengal	Dye that are made of spices, earth, soot, etc.
Madhubani painting	Madhubani (Bihar)	Mud coated wall, cloth paper
Miniature painting	Developed during Mughal Period i.e. 16th – 19th century	precious stones conch shells, gold and silver
Tanjore art	Tanjore (Southern Tamil Nadu)	Semi-precious stones, glass and gold
Kalamkari	Golkonda and Chennai and Masulipatnam area of Hyderabad	pens made of bamboo and natural colours extracted from vegetables
Warli Painting	North Sahyadri Range in India.	Rice paste, mix with Gum and Water Red clay (Geru), cow dung, mud
Gond art	Gond Tribes of Central India.	Made on walls, ceilings and floors of village houses

Famous Indian Painters

Rabindranath Tagore	7 May 1861 – 7 Aug 1941
Abanindranath Tagore	7 Aug 1871 – 5 Dec 1951
Amrita Sher-Gil	30 Jan 1913 – 5 Dec 1941
Jamini Roy	1 Apr 1887 – 24 Apr 1972
Francis Newton Souza	12 Apr 1924 -28 Mar 2002
S.H. Raza	22 Feb 1922 - 23 june 2016
Tyeb Mehta	25 Jul 1925 – 2 Jul 2009
Satish Gujral	25 Dec 1925 - Till date
Nandalal Bose	3 Dec 1882 – 16 Apr 1966
Manjit Bawa	1941-29 Dec 2008
M. F. Husain	17 Sep 1915 – 9 Jun 2011

Legends of Indian Music

Legends	Life Span	Forte	Awards
Pandit Ravi Shankar	7 April 1920 – 11 Dec 2012	Sitar	Magsaysay award, Padma Vibhushan, UNESCO International Music,
Pandit Hariprasad Chaurasia	1st July 1938	Bansuri	Sangeet Natak Academy, Padma Bhushan, Konark Samman, Yash,
Pandit Shivkumar Sharma	13-1-1938	Santoor	Sangeet Natak Akademi Award, Padma Vibhushan, Padma Shri
Ustad Amjad Ali Khan	9-10-1945	Sarod	UNESCO Award, Padma Vibhusha, Unicef's National Ambassadorship,
Ustad Bismillah Khan	21-3-1913 to 21-8-2006	Shehnai	Bharat Ratna, Fellow of Sangeet Natak Akademi, Padma Vibhushan
Ustad Zakir Hussain	9-3-1951	Tabla	P. Bhushan, Grammy, Sangeet Natak Akademi.
Pandit Bhimsen Gururaj Joshi	4-2-1922 to 24-1-2011	Indian classical vocalist	Sangeet Natak Akademi P. Vibhushan,
Pandit Jasraj	28-1-1930	Indian classical vocalist	P. Vibhushan, Sangeet Natak Akademi
M. S. Subbulakshmi	16-7-1916 to 11-12-2004	Classical vocalist	Sangeet Natak Akademi Ramon Magsaysay, P. Vibhushan
Dr. Lakshminarayana Subramaniam	23 July 1947-	Classical, Carnatic,	Lifetime Achievement GiMA ISKCON,
M.Balamurali Krishna	6 July 1930-	Carnatic music	Padma Vibhushan, Padma Bhushan,
Bade Ghulam Ali Khan	2 April 1902 – 25 April 1968	Sarangi,	NA

Indian Dance

There are many types of dance forms in India which are deeply religious in content to those which are performed on small occasions. The Indian dances are broadly divided into Classical dances and folk dances.

The most popular classical dance styles of India are **Bharatnatyam** of Tamil Nadu, **Kathakali** and **Mohiniattam** of Kerala, **Odissi** of Odisha, **Kathak** of Uttar Pradesh, **Kuchipudi** of Andhra Pradesh and **Manipuri** of Manipur.

Theatres

The rich Indian theater culture has its origin dates back in first century, CE, and started and nurtured by the society as means of expressing, communicating and sharing the ideas-opinions-emotions-believe of mankind.

Some of the Important Theatres of Modern India

Name	Founder	Year and Place of Establishment	People Associated with it
National School of Drama (Deemed University)	Ministry of Culture, Government of India.	1959, New Delhi	Naseeruddin Shah, Irfan Khan, Anupam Kher, Nawazuddin Siddiqui, Pankaj Kapur, Himani Shivpuri and many more

Bhartendu Academy of Dramatic Arts	Padma Shri Raj Bisaria.	1975, Lucknow,	Rajiv Jain, Raajpal Yadav, Anupam Shyam
Theatre Arts Workshop (TAW)	Raj Bisaria	1966, Lucknow	

Tourism

India has become a popular tourist destination with thousands of people visiting different parts of India each year. Major tourist destinations in India are the Himalayas, Agra, Jaipur, Goa, Kerala, Delhi, Odisha and Maharshtra.

Famous Tourist Destination in India

Akshardham Temple:

The 108 feet tall temple was built on 2nd, November 1992 in memory of Pramukh Swami in Gandhinagar district of Gujarat.

Ajmer Sharif:

It is sufi shrine dedicated to the sufi saint Moinuddin Chishti. It is situated in Ajmer, Rajasthan.

Amarnath Cave:

It is situated in Jammu and Kashmir

Ajanta and Ellora Caves:

They contain a cluster of Hindu and Jain temples along with cave monuments in.

Dal Lake:

The enchanting lake of Jammu and Kasmir bordered by ice covered mountains from three sides is famous for its gardens, shikara rides and house boat stay.

Golden Temple:

Harmandir Sahib Gurudwara, is commonly called as Golden Temple in Amritsar Punjab.

Gateway of India:

It is made by British in 1914 in Mumbai.

Haji Ali Dargah: The very famous dargah (tomb) is located on an islet of the coast of Worli in the Southern part of Mumbai built in 1431 in the memory of a wealthy merchant Sayyed Peer Haji Ali Shah Bukhari.

Khajuraho Group of Monuments: It is a group of Hindu and Jain temples situated in Madhya Pradesh.

Mahabaleshwar: It is a vast magnificent plateau located at a distance of 120 km south west of Pune with an average height of 1353 meters.

Taj Mahal: It is a white marble mausoleum located on the southern bank of the Yamuna river inAgra, Uttar Pradesh. It was built by Shah Jahan in 1632 in the memory of his loving wife Mumtaz Mahal.

Vaishno Devi Temple, Jammu Kashmir: The temple is recognized as one of the "Shakti Peeths" of goddess Durga. The holy shrine is situated in the folds of mighty 'Tirkuta' Hills' which attracts lakhs of devotees from all parts of India and abroad

Indian Film Industry

India is the largest producer of films in the world and second oldest film industry in the world which originated around about 103 years ago. It was in early 1913 that an Indian film received a public screening. The film was **Raja Harischandra**. Its director, Dadasaheb Phalke. By the mid 1920s, Madras had become the epicentre for all film related activities. Raghupathi Venkaiah Naidu, SS Vasan, AV Meiyappan set up production houses in Madras to shoot Telugu and Tamil films.

The silent era came to an end when Ardeshir Irani produced his first talkie, **'Alam Ara'** in 1931. If **Phalke** was the **father of Indian cinema**, **Irani** was the **father of the talkie**. The first talkie films in Bengali (**Jumai Shasthi**), Telugu (**Bhakta Prahlad**) and Tamil (**Kalidass**) were released in the same year.

Largest film industry in India is the Hindi film industry mostly concentrated in Mumbai (Bombay), and is commonly referred to as "Bollywood". Kochi and Kolkata are commonly referred to as "Tollywood"(Telugu), "Kollywood"(Tamil), "Sandalwood"(Kannada), "Mollywood"(Malayalam),"Tollywood"(Bangla). The largest film studio complex in the world is **Ramoji Film City** is located at Hyderabad , India, which was opened in 1996 and measures 674 ha (1,666 acres). Comprising 47 sound stages.

Communication, Transport, News & Media

Communication

Post Office

- The Department of Posts was founded in India on 1st April, 1774.
- This department serves as an agent of Govt.

Telecommunication

- Communication technology uses channels to transmit information (as electrical signals), either over a physical medium (such as signal cables), or in the form of electromagnetic waves.
- The Telecommunications system in India is the 2nd largest in the world. The construction of 4,000 miles (6,400 km) of telegraph lines was started in November 1853.
- Code division multiple access (CDMA) is a channel access method used by various radio communication technologies.
- 4G, is the fourth generation of mobile telecommunications technology, succeeding 3G.

Communications Satellite

- A communications satellite is an artificial satellite that relays and amplifies radio telecommunications signals via a transponder; it creates a communication channel between a source transmitter and a receiver(s) at different locations on Earth.
- Communications satellites are used for television, telephone, radio, internet, and military applications.

Transport

Indian Road Network

- India has a road network of over approx. 4,689,842 kilometers.
- The Central Government is responsible for development and maintenance of the National Highways system.
- The Ministry carries out development and maintenance work of National Highways through three agencies. viz. National Highways Authority of India (NHAI), State Public Works Department (PWDs) and Border Road Organization (BRO).

Quick Facts

Categories	Dimensions in Kms (up to 2011)	Responsible Authority
National Highways	92,851	Ministry of Road Transport and Highways (Central government)
State Highways	1,63,898	State governments (State's public works department)
Major and Other District Roads	17,05,706	Local governments, Panchayats and Municipalities
Rural Roads	27,49,805	Local governments, Panchayats and Municipalities

National Highways Development Projects

Golden Quadrilateral : It comprises construction of 5,846 km long 4/6 lane, high density traffic corridor, to connect India's four big metro cities of Delhi-Mumbai-Chennai and Kolkata.

North-South and East-West Corridors: North-South corridor aims at connecting Srinagar in Jammu and Kashmir with Kaniyakumari in Tamil Nadu (including Kochchi-Salem Spur) with 4,076 km long road. The East-West Corridor has been planned to connect Silchar in Assam with the port town of Porbandar in Gujarat with 3,640 km of road length.

Important National Highways

NH	Connects
NH 1	New Delhi-Ambala-Jalandhar-Amritsar
NH 2	Delhi-Mathura-Agra-Kanpur- Allahabad-Varanasi-Kolkata
NH 3	Agra-Gwalior-Nasik-Mumbai
NH 4	Thane and Chennai via Pune and Belgaum
NH 5	Kolkata-Chennai
NH 6	Kolkata-Dhule
NH 7	Varanasi-Kanyakumari
NH 8	Delhi-Mumbai (via Jaipur, Boroda & Ahmedabad)
NH 9	Mumbai-Vijaywada
NH 10	Delhi-Fazilka
NH 24	Delhi - Lucknow
NH 26	Lucknow-Varanasi

Indian Railways

Indian Railways is a state-owned enterprise and one of the world's largest railway networks comprising 115,000 km of track over a route of 65,808 km and 7,112 stations. It was founded on April 16, 1853.

Top Ten Countries with Longest Rail Network in the World

Rank	Country	Route Km.
1.	USA	250000
2.	China	100000
3.	Russia	85500
4.	**India**	**65000**
5.	Canada	48000
6.	Germany	41000
7.	Australia	40000
8.	Argentina	36000
9.	France	29000
10.	Brazil	28000

Bangaluru Metro: Bengaluru Metro also known as Namma Metro is recently started rapid transit rail system in the Bengaluru city of Karnataka.

Jaipur Metro: The pink city of Rajasthan is got its first metro line of 9.2 km from Mansarovar to Chandpole Bazaar in November 2010.

Aviation Industry

Air transport in India made a beginning in 1911 when airmail operation commenced over a distance of 10 km between Allahabad and Naini. The Airport Authority of India was constituted in 1972.

- JRD Tata was the first licensed pilot of Federation aeronautique International on behalf of the Aero Club of India and Burma.
- Prem Mathur became the first female commercial pilot to start flying for Deccan Airways, as she obtained her commercial pilots licence in 1947.

> 5/20 rule : The rule allows an Indian carrier to fly abroad only after it has completed five years of domestic operations and maintains a fleet of 20 aircrafts.

Water Ways

India has 14,500 km of navigable waterways. At present, 5,685 km of major rivers are navigable. The Inland Waterways Authority was set up in 1986.

National Waterways of India

Waterways	Stretch	Specification
NW 1	Allahabad-Haldia stretch (1,620 km)	It is divided into three parts for developmental purposes– (i) Haldia- Farakka (560 km), (ii) Farakka-Patna (460 km), (iii) Patna- Allahabad (600 km).
NW 2	Sadiya-Dhubri stretch (891 km)	Brahmaputra is navigable by steamers up to Dibrugarh (1,384 km) which is shared by India `and Bangladesh.
NW 3	Kottapuram-Kollam stretch (205 km)	It includes 168 km of west coast canal along with Champakara canal (23 km) and Udyogmandal canal (14 km).
NW 4	Specified streches of Godavari and Krishna rivers along with Kakinada Puducherry stretch of canals (1078 km)	
NW 5	Specified stretches of river Brahmani along with Matai river, delta channels of Mahanadi and Brahmani rivers and East Coast canals (588km).	

Ports

Indian coastline is about 7516.6 kilometers and it is one of the biggest peninsulas in the world. It is serviced by 12 major ports, 200 notified minor and intermediate ports. Maharashtra (48) has the maximum and Gujarat (42) and Andaman & Nicobar Islands (23).

The Coastal States in India are Andhra Pradesh, Odisha, West Bengal, Tamil Nadu, Kerala, Karnataka, Goa, Maharashtra and Gujarat.

Name of the Port	Coast	State
Kandla	Western Coast	Gujarat
Mumbai	Western Coast	Maharashtra
Jawaharlal Nehru	Western Coast	Maharashtra
Mormugao	Western Coast	Goa
Manglore	Western Coast	Karnataka
Kochi	Western Coast	Kerala
Haldia	Eastern Coast	West Bengal
Paradip	Eastern Coast	Odisha
Vishakapatnam	Eastern Coast	Andhra Pradesh
Chennai	Eastern Coast	Tamil Nadu
Ennore	Eastern Coast	Tamil Nadu
Tutikorin	Eastern Coast	Tamil Nadu

News & Media

Newspaper

Newspaper is the print media which prints information, activities and daily occurrences around us. It was introduced in 1780.

Registrar of Newspapers is a statutory body of Government of India which is popularly known as RNI. It was established on 1st July 1956.

Press Trust of India (PTI) was incorporated in Madras on, 27th August, 1947.

United News of India (UNI) was founded on December 1961under the company acts. However its commercial application started on 21st March 1961.

Prasar Bharti is an autonomous body set up by an Act of Parliament on 23 Nov, 1997.

All India Radio (AIR) or Akashwani was formed in 1930 as a part of Prasar Bharti.

Doordarshan was launched on 15 September, 1959 as a part of Prasar Bharti with the motto Satyam Shivam Sundaram.

Indian Railways

History and Important facts of Railways

- The first train in India was run between Mumbai and Thane on 16th April 1853.
- The second train in India was run in 1854 in between Howrah and Hoogly.
- Indian Railway Board was established in 1905, And the headquarters of Indian Railways is situated in New Delhi.
- The Indian Railway was nationalised in 1950AD.
- Indian Railways has the First Position in Asian Nations and Fourth in the world.
- The first electric train in India is "Deccan Queen", it was introduced in 1929 in between Mumbai and Pune.
- Indian Railway is the largest Public sector Enterprises in the country.
- Indian railway has the second biggest electrified system in the world after Russia.
- The faster Train in India is Train 18 or Vande Bharat Expresss that was flagged off by Prime Minister Narendra Modi on 15th February 2019, from the New Delhi railway station.
- Vande Bharat Express will travel from **Delhi** to **Varanasi** in **9 hours and 45 minutes,** with stoppage points at **Kanpur** and Prayagraj.
- Vande Bharat Express can run up to a maximum speed of 160 km/hour.
- The train had been produced indigenously at the Integral Coach Factory, Chennai in 18 months.
- The route covered (track length) by Indian Railways is 119,630 km. of total track.
- The total number of Railways Stations in India is 7216.
- Deen Dayal Upadhyaya Yard is the largest Railway Yard of Indian Railway.
- The longest Railway Platform in India is at Gorakhpur (Uttar Pradesh)with a length of 1366.33meter.
- Maximum Number of Trains from different parts of the country departs fromMumbai.
- Dhanbad (The Coal Capital of India) is the 2nd Highest Fright Revenue Generating Stations in India, comes after Mumbai. Mumbai Topped in the lists in Frights Revenue Generation.
- The "Vivek Express (Dibrugarh – Kanyakumari)" is the longest Route train which covers Dibrugarh in Assam, North-East India to Kanyakumari, Tamil Nadu which is the southernmost tip of Mainland India.
- The second longest train in the country is "Himsagar Express" which runs between Jammu Tawi to Kanyakumari covers a total route of 3726Kilometers and passes through Ten States.
- The First Metro Rail was introduced on 24th October 1984 between Dumdum and Belgachhia Railway stations in Kolkata (West Bengal). Currently 8 states in India have Metro Rail Facility in the Country.
- The First Metro train in World started in London (UK).
- The longest Railway Tunnel in India is Located in Pir Panjal Range of Himalayas in Jammu and Kashmir which is 11km long.
- Eastern Railway is the Largest and Hi-Tech Railway Zones in India whereas Western Railway is the Busiest Railway Zone. [You will see Northern Zone is longest Railway Zones in Many websites but its 100% Wrong.]
- First Railway Bridge in India was Dapoorie Viaduct between Mumbai-Thane route
- First Railway Tunnel in India was –Parsik Tunnel
- World's Longest Railway Route is Trans Siberian Railways
- India's First Computerized Railway Reservation Started in New Delhi in 1986.
- Railway Staff Colleges is Located at Barodara (Baroda).

Facts About Railway Tracks

According to distance between the Railways Lines, there are three systems operating in the Country.

- Broad Gauge – Distance 1.67m
- Meter Gauge – Distance 1.00m
- Narrow Gauge – Distance 0.762 or 0.610 m

Railway Manufacturing Units

- Chittaranjan Locomotive Works (CLW) – It is situated in Chittaranjan (W.B). It manufactures electric engines.
- Diesel Locomotive Works (DLW) – It is Situated at Varanasi and Manufactures Diesel Engines.
- Integral Coach Factory – Situated at Perambur (Chennai) and manufactures Rail Coaches.

- Wheel and Axel Plant – Situated at Yalahka (Bangalore) and manufactures wheel and axels.
- Diesel Component Works – Situated at Patiala(Punjab) and manufactures components of diesel engines.
- Rail Coach Factory – Situated at Kapurthala (Punjab) and manufactures Railway Coaches.
- Konkan Rail Project (Konkan Railway) – This is the joint venture of the government of Maharashtra, Goa and Karnataka and Kerala. Under this Project a Railway Lines joining Mumbai and Mangalore(Karnataka) has been laid down.

Important Railway Committees

- Shahnawaz Committee – 1954, High Level Safety Review Committee
- Kanjaru Committee – 1962, Railway Accidents Committee
- Wahchoo Committee – 1968, Railway Safety Committee
- Seekari Committee – 1978, Railway Accidents Enquiry Committee
- Khanna Committee – 1998, Railway Safety Review Committee
- Arvind Panagariya committee – 2016 to fast-track bullet train project

INDIAN RAILWAY'S ZONE'S & THEIR DIVISIONS WITH HEAQUARTERS

Sl.No.	Name of the Zone(HQ)	Divisions
1	Central Railway (MUMBAI)	Bhusawal, Nagpur, Mumbai(CST)*, Solapur*, Pune^
2	Eastern Railway (KOLKATA)	Malda, Howarh, Sealdah, Asansol
3	Northern Railway (NEW DELHI)	Ambala, Ferozpur, Lucknow, Moradabad, Delhi
4	North Eastern Railway (GORAKHPUR)	Lucknow, Varanasi, Izatnagar*
5	Northeast Frontier Railway (GUWAHATI)	Katihar, Lumding, Tinsukhia, Alipurduar*, Rangiya^
6	Southern Railway (CHENNAI)	Chennai, Madurai, Palghat, Trichy, Trivandrum
7	South Central Railway (SECUNDERABAD)*	Secunderabad*, Hyderabad*, Guntakal*, Vijaywada*, Guntur^, Nanded^
8	South Eastern Railway (KOLKATA)	Kharagpur, Chakradharpur*, Adra*, Ranchi^
9	Western Railway (MUMBAI)	Bhavnagar, Mumbai Central, Ratlam*, Rajkot*, Vadodara*, Ahemdabad^
10	East Central Railway (HAJIPUR)**	Danapur, Dhanbad, Sonepur, Mughalsarai, Samastipur
11	East Coast Railway (BHUBANESWAR)^*	Khurda Road, Waltair, Sambalpur
12	North Central Railway (ALLAHABAD)^	Allahabad*, Jhansi*, Agra^
13	North Western Railway (JAIPUR)**	Bikaner*, Jodhpur, Jaipur*, Ajmer*
14	South East Central Railway (BILASPUR)^	Nagpur, Bilaspur*, Raipur^
15	South Western Railway (HUBLI)^	Bangalore, Mysore, Hubli*
16	West Central Railway (JABALPUR)^	Jabalpur, Bhopal, Kota*
17	Kolkata Metro Railway	Kolkata

* New Railway Zone at Vishakja Patnam and a new division with headquarters at Rayagada has been approved by Union Cabinet. After this SCR and East Coast Railway will be recoganized.

Sports

Olympics

- The **first Modern Olympics** Games were started in **Athens** on **6th April 1896**. The Olympics games originated in the City of **Olympia** of Greece in 776 B.C.
  The Olympic flag was created in **1914** at the suggestion of **Baron Pierre de Coubertin** and was hoisted first time in the Antwerp Olympic Games in **1920**. It is made up of **white silk** and contains **five intertwined rings** as the **Olympics** emblem.
- The Colour of rings represents different continents as given below:

Blue	-	Europe
Yellow	-	Asia
Black	-	Africa
Red	-	America
Green	-	Australia & Oceania

- The **Olympic motto** is "Citius – Altius – Fortius" (Faster, higher, Stronger)
- **Mary Leela Rao** was the 1st Indian woman participant in The Olympic Games

Commonwealth Games

- It is held every **4th** year in between the Olympic years.
- The first Commonwealth Games was held in **1930** at **Hamilton**, Canada.
- **India**, for the first time, participated in the 2nd Commonwealth Games held in **1934** in **London**.

Asian Games

- The idea of the Asian Games was first conceived by **Prof. G.D. Sondhi**. The first Asian Games were held at **New Delhi** on 4 March **1951**.
- The **motto** of the Asian Games "**Play the game in Spirit of the game**" was given by **Pt. J.L Nehru**.

- Its emblem is a bright full rising **Sun** with interlocking **rings**.
- 17th Asian Games was held in **Incheon (South Korea)** in **2014**.
- **18th** will be held in **Jakarta** (Indonesia) in **2018**.

South Asian Games

- South Asian Games (SAG) was first held in **1984** at **Kathmandu**, Nepal. The eight participating Countries are Afghanistan, Bangladesh, Bhutan, India, Maldives, Nepal, Pakistan, Sri Lanka.
- The last SAG was held in 2016 at Hambantota, Sri Lanka.

Cricket World Cup

- It is organised by the International Cricket Council (ICC) after every 4 years.
- The first World Cup was organized in **England** in June **1975**.
- Australia is the Champion of ICC Cricket World Cup 2015.
- The next World Cup is scheduled in 2019 in England.

FIFA World Cup

- **Germany** was The Champion of 20th FIFA world cup held in 2014 in Brazil.
- **Brazil** has won five times and they are the only team to have played in every tournament.
- The next two World Cups will be hosted by **Russia** in 2018 and **Qatar** in 2022.

Hockey World Cup

- It was started in **1971**.
- Indian has won the tournament only once in **1975**.
- The last Hockey World Cup was held in **2014** in **Hague**, Netherlands whose winner was Australia.

- The next tournament is scheduled in **2018** to be held in **Bhubaneswar**, India.

IPL 2016

- It is a professional Twenty 20 Cricket league in India (BCCI).
- The ninth and the latest IPL was held in 2016. The Sun risers Hyderabad were crowned as the champion after they won against Royal Challengers Bangalore in the Finals.

Trophies and Sports

National

Name of the Trophy	Related game
Aga Khan Cup	Hockey
Barna Bellack Cup	Table Tennis
Beighton Cup	Hockey
Bombay Gold Cup	Hockey
Burdwan Trophy	Weight Lifting
D.C.M. Trophy	Football
Dhyan Chand Trophy	Hockey
Dr. B.C. Roy Trophy	Football
Duleep Trophy	Cricket
Durand Cup	Football
Ezra Cup	Polo
I.F.A Shield	Football
Lady Ratan Tata Trophy	Hockey
Moin ud daula Gold Cup	Cricket
Rangaswami Cup	Hockey
Ranji Trophy	Cricket
Santosh Trophy	Football
Scindia Gold Cup	Hockey
Subroto Mukherjee Cup	Football (Inter-School)
Wellington Trophy	Rowing

International

Name of the Trophy	Related game
Nehru Trophy	Hockey
American Cup	Yatch Racing
Ashes Cup	Cricket (Australia-England)
Azlan Shah	Hockey
US Masters	Golf
Hopman Cup	Lawn Tennis
Colombo Cup Trophy	Football
Davis Cup	Lawn Tennis
Kings Cup Race	Air Races (England)
Merdeka Cup	Football (Asia)
Thomas Cup	World Badminton (Men)
Uber Cup	World Badminton (women)
US-Open	Lawn Tennis
French-Open	Lawn Tennis
Australian Open	Lawn Tennis
Wimbledon	Lawn Tennis
Masters Champions Trophy	Hockey
British Open	Golf
Malaysian Open	Badminton
Tata Open	Lawn Tennis

Number of Players on each side

Badminton	1 or 2	Polo	4
Baseball	9	Rugby Football	15
Basketball	5	Tennis and Table tennis	1 or 2
Cricket	11	Water Polo	7
Football	11	Volleyball	6
Hockey	11	Kabaddi	7
Chess	1		

Terms in Sports and Games

Badminton   Deuce, Double, Drop, Fault, Game, Let, Love, Smash.

Baseball   Bunt, Diamond, Home, Pitcher, Put out, Strike.

Billiards   Break, Cannons, Cue, In off, Jigger, Scratch,

Boat Race   Cox

Boxing	Hook, Jab, Knock-out, Punch, Upper cut.
Chess	Check, Checkmate, Gambit, Stalemate
Cricket	Bowling, Bouncer, Crease, Cover point, Drive, Duck, Follow on, Googly, Gulley, Hat Trick, Hit wicket, L.B.W. (Leg Before Wicket), Leg Break, Leg spinner, Leg bye Maiden over, No ball, Pitch, Run, Silly point, Stumped, Wicket keeper.
Football	Dribble, Drop Kick, Foul, Hattrick, Off-side, Penalty, Throw in, Touch Down.
Golf	Bogey, Caddie, Hole, Links, Put, Putting the green, Stymie, Tee.
Hockey	Bull, Carry, Centre Forward, Carried, Dribble, Goal, Hat trick, Penalty corner, Scoop, Short corner, Sticks, Striking circle, Under cutting.
Horse Racing	Jockey, Place, Protest, Punter, Win.
Lawn Tennis	Back-hand-drive, Service, Smash, Volley, Deuce, Game, Set, Love.
Polo	Bunder, Chuckker, Mallet.
Rifle Shooting	Bull's eye.
Swimming	Stroke.
Volley ball	Booster, Deuce, Love, Service, Spikers.
Wrestling	Half Nelson, Heave.